Daily Reflections

Compiled by
the Daughters of St. Paul

ST. PAUL EDITIONS

NIHIL OBSTAT:
   Rev. Richard V. Lawlor, S.J.

IMPRIMATUR:
   ✠ Humberto Cardinal Medeiros
   Archbishop of Boston

Library of Congress Cataloging in Publication Data

Daily Reflections.
      1. Devotional calendars—Catholic Church.
I. Daughters of St. Paul.

BV4810.D26   242'.2   81-19555

ISBN 0-8198-1803-8 cloth   AACR2
      0-8198-1804-6 paper

Printed in U.S.A. by the Daughters of St. Paul
50 St. Paul's Ave., Boston, MA 02130

The Daughters of St. Paul are an international congregation of religious women serving the Church with the communications media.

CONTENTS

INTRODUCTION

Each passing year is filled with opportunities to grow closer to God.

Daily Reflections presents, for each day of the year, a short thought—mainly from the writings of the Saints—reflection, and prayer, which aim at inspiring, uplifting and encouraging. Amid today's fast-paced modern society, *Daily Reflections* offers the opportunity to pause and ponder those realities which never pass away.

A treasury of brief meditations that will add new dimension and depth to one's spiritual life.

JANUARY
The Will of God

January 1

Feast of the Solemnity of Mary, the Mother of God—"The blessed Virgin is the true Mother of God. Thus she had a certain unique right to be obeyed by the Incarnate Son of God. Wondrous thing that a creature command the Creator! She had a certain unique right to the love which every son owes to his mother.... Hence, at the wedding at Cana, even though Jesus Christ affirmed that His hour had not yet come, Mary requested the miracle, and it was worked."   *James Alberione*

Reflection — *"Through obedience we give God the best we have: our will. Through disobedience, however, we deprive God of the greatest homage He expects from us.*

Prayer — "You are my Mother, O Virgin Mary. Keep me safe lest I ever offend your dear Son, and obtain for me the grace to please Him always and in all things."   *James Alberione*

January 2

"I always do what is pleasing to him [the Father]" (Jn. 8:29). The sole program of Jesus' life was to do the will of His Father, and He told His disciples: "If you continue in my word, you are truly my disciples, and you will know the truth, and the truth will make you free" (Jn. 8:31).

Reflection — *Let us remember the words of Samuel: "Obedience is better than sacrifice..." (1 Sm. 15:22).* "We will make progress in sanctity according to the degree to which we have conquered our own will."*   James Alberione

Prayer — "Teach me to do your will, for you are my God" (Ps. 143:10).*

January 3

"God created us to know, love and serve Him in this world, and to enjoy Him forever in Paradise."
                                           Catechism of Pope St. Pius X

Reflection — *"Only what helps us to serve God is lasting, the rest is smoke."*   St. Jerome

Prayer — Frequently repeat during the day: "Lord, what do you will for me to do?" (cf. Acts 22:10)

January 4

"The words 'I will not serve' belong to the devil; but the words 'Here I am' are the watchwords of those who love Jesus."   Timothy Giaccardo

Reflection — *"Eye has not seen, ear has not heard,
nor has it so much as dawned on man
what God has prepared for those who love him"
(1 Cor. 2:9)**

*Let us show our love for Jesus by accepting His
will in our everyday life.*

Prayer — *"O Lord, my allotted portion and my
cup,
you it is who hold fast my lot.
You will show me the path to life,
fullness of joys in your presence,
the delights at your right hand forever"
(Ps. 16:5, 11).**

January 5

"Those who do the will of God never go to hell;
those who refuse to do His will never go to
heaven." *St. Alphonsus Liguori*

Reflection — *"Always desire and pray that the will
of God be perfectly fulfilled in you."* Imitation of Christ

Prayer — My God, I adore Your holy, eternal and
unfathomable designs. I submit to them with all
my heart for love of You, so that everything You
want or permit to happen will result in Your
greater glory and my sanctification. Amen.

January 6

"A single drop of obedience to the will of God
is worth more than a vessel full of any other
virtue." *St. Mary Magdalene de Pazzi*

"Obedience to the little rules is often a greater sign of fidelity than obedience in big things."

Timothy Giaccardo

Reflection — *"Obey...with the reverence, the awe, and the sincerity you owe to Christ.... Do God's will with your whole heart as slaves of Christ. Give your service willingly, doing it for the Lord rather than men" (Eph. 6:5-7).* *

Prayer — Draw us to You, Jesus, so that by following in Your footsteps, we will come to possess You forever in heaven.

January 7

"Children, obey your parents in the Lord, for that is what is expected of you" (Eph. 6:1).*

Reflection — *" 'Honor your father and mother' is the first commandment to carry a promise with it—'that it may go well with you, and that you may have long life on the earth' " (Eph. 6:2-3).* *

Prayer — Master, show us the treasures of Your wisdom, let us know the Father, make us Your true disciples.

January 8

"Defer to one another out of reverence for Christ. Wives should be submissive to their husbands as if to the Lord because the husband is head of his wife just as Christ is head of his body the church.... As the church submits to Christ, so wives should submit to their husbands in everything" (Eph. 5:21-24).*

Reflection — *"A gracious woman wins esteem, but she who hates virtue is covered with shame" (Prv. 11:16).* *

Prayer — Lord, You created everything for us, as we are for Christ. Lead us not into temptation, but deliver us from the danger of abusing the gifts You gave us with such wisdom and love.

January 9

"My son, forget not my teaching,
  keep in mind my commands;
For many days, and years of life,
  and peace, will they bring you" (Prv. 3:1-2). *

Reflection — *"Happy the man who obeys me, and happy those who keep my ways....
For he who finds me finds life, and wins favor from the Lord" (Prv. 8:33-35).* *

Prayer — O Virgin Mary, radiant with joy, grant that we may believe in the happiness which God in His love wills to offer us. Teach us to detach ourselves from worldly pleasures and to seek our happiness in God.

January 10

Oh, what wonder and joy Mary experienced when she heard the words: Hail, full of grace, the Lord is with you!... You will conceive in your womb and bear a son, and you shall call his name Jesus (cf. Lk. 1:30-31).

Reflection — *Her humble and prompt reply to the will of God was: "Behold, I am the handmaid of the Lord; let it be to me according to your word" (Lk. 1:38).*

Prayer — Father, Your will be done on earth as it is in heaven.

January 11

"If daily we live according to God's intention and designs, we will be able to exclaim as we look back at the point of death: 'It is consummated!' Lord, what You wanted of me, I have done: I have corresponded to my vocation in life; I have done Your will! It will be a real consolation, a pledge of paradise."   *James Alberione*

Reflection — *"If we do God's will in life, we will have such comfort in death."*   *James Alberione*

Prayer — Lord, my Creator and Redeemer, I wholeheartedly accept everything from Your Fatherly hands, in a spirit of adoration, and to merit heaven.

January 12

"It is much more useful for our sanctification for us to perform little tasks under obedience than to do great things through our own will."
    St. Stanislaus Kostka

Reflection — *"Let us ask to die after having corresponded so faithfully to our vocation in life that we* *will be able to say: 'I have done what the Lord wished of me. I have accomplished His will.' "*

James Alberione

Prayer — O divine Holy Spirit, to You I consecrate my will. Guide me in Your will; sustain me in the observance of the commandments, in the fulfillment of my duties.

January 13

"Jesus said to them, 'My food is to do the will of him who sent me...' " (Jn. 4:34).

Reflection — *Jesus was the most perfect model of obedience to the will of God.*

Prayer — O Jesus, Model of holiness, make me Your faithful imitator.

January 14

"If any one is a worshiper of God and does his will, God listens to him" (Jn. 9:31).

Reflection — *Let us make the prayer of Jesus our own: "...not my will, but yours be done" (Lk. 22:42).* *

Prayer — "Father, into your hands I commend my spirit" (Lk. 23:46).*

January 15

"Mary had but one word to say throughout her life: *yes.* And she repeated it still on Calvary: *Behold the handmaid of the Lord, may it be done unto me according to His will, as it pleases Him.*"

James Alberione

Reflection — *"If substantially we have accomplished the will of God, despite the imperfections of weakness, then we will have the reward."*

James Alberione

Prayer — O Mary, to you I consecrate my entire life. Pray for me now and in the final battle at the hour of my death.

January 16

"Let us recognize the goodness and the love of God the Savior, who, condescending to our misery, so remote from His infinite sanctity, wished to make it easier for us to imitate His holiness by giving us as a model the human person of His Mother. She, in fact, among human beings, offers the most shining example and the closest to us, of that perfect obedience whereby we lovingly and readily conform with the will of the eternal Father."

Pope Paul VI

Reflection — *"[Let us] have these habitual dispositions, this internal preparation to do the will of God at all times, so that God may do with us whatever He pleases, without finding resistance in our heart, in our life, in our will."*

James Alberione

Prayer — *"Remember, Virgin Mary, the sorrow that pierced you when you sought Jesus for three days and found Him in the temple. Grant that we may long for Christ and seek Him always and everywhere. Crown our search with success."*

James Alberione

January 17

"When one loves his own will and is attached to his own opinions, then, when confronted with the will of God, he feels repugnance and adapts himself unwillingly, out of force. But God repays only what is done in accordance with His will. Then, and only then, the reward is very great."

James Alberione

Reflection — *"If we are already prepared to say our yes to the Lord, then when the time comes we will say, with generosity, joy and great faith: "The will of God be done."* *James Alberione*

Prayer — Not my will, but Yours be done, O Lord.

January 18

"Behold the most painful *yes* that she [Mary] said after Jesus was taken down from the cross: *It is pleasing to the Lord; it is pleasing also to me.* Christ Himself, as we well know, made this full closeness to the approval of the Father the supreme ideal of His human behavior, declaring: 'I do always the things that are pleasing to him.' "

Pope Paul VI

Reflection — *"How are our interior dispositions? Are we well disposed in everything, or do we have preferences? Am I disposed to accept sickness as well as health? A life long or short? Criticism or praise? Do I consider myself a true servant of God? This is how the Blessed Virgin considered herself—a handmaid of God."* *James Alberione*

Prayer — "Remember, Virgin Mary, the sorrow you felt when Jesus, wrapped in linen, was placed in the sepulcher. Cleanse our soul with the most precious blood of your Son, and at the final moments of our life, instill in us sentiments of repentance, of faith, of hope, and of love, and then open to us the gates of heaven."   *James Alberione*

January 19

"Holiness consists in conformity to the divine will. And it is realized in the continual and exact fulfillment of one's duties of state in life."

Pope Benedict XIV

Reflection — *"Let us take care not to form strange or vague concepts of holiness. Sanctity lies only in conformity to the will of God, whether one be the Pope or a street cleaner, a superior or a subject."*

James Alberione

Prayer — "Glory in his holy name;
  rejoice, O hearts that seek the Lord!
Look to the Lord in his strength;
  seek to serve him constantly" (Ps. 105:3-4).*

January 20

"The will must bow before God, our Creator and last End. There are some who place their own will before God's will. Sin is always a disobedience to God's law, to His commandments. The root of all sin is disobedience to God's will."   *James Alberione*

Reflection — *Let us ponder and take courage in Jesus' words to His disciples: "Take my yoke upon you, and learn from me; for I am gentle and lowly in* *heart, and you will find rest for your souls. For my yoke is easy, and my burden is light" (Mt. 11:29-30).*

Prayer — "Happy are they who observe what is right,
   who do always what is just.
Remember me, O Lord, as you favor
   your people;
   visit me with your saving help..." (Ps. 106:3-4).*

January 21

"Sanctity is a stubbornness about fulfilling God's will always and in spite of any difficulty whatsoever."
                                        James Alberione

Reflection — *Jesus has promised the kingdom of heaven to those who do God's will: "Not everyone who says to me, 'Lord, Lord,' shall enter the kingdom of heaven, but he who does the will of my Father who is in heaven" (Mt. 7:21).*

Prayer — Jesus Master, inspire us with thoughts of faith, peace, moderation, thrift, so that, together with our daily bread, we will always seek spiritual goods and heaven.

January 22

"At times it costs to do the will of God because it is a bit contrary to ours; and we ask: Why does the Lord permit that? Why does He permit this or that other? It is because He knows what is good for us."   *Servant of God, Mother Thecla Merlo*

Reflection — *"If we always do well what God wants, we unite ourselves intimately to Him already in this life, and then we will be more perfectly united with Him in heaven."*

Servant of God, Mother Thecla Merlo

Prayer — Lord, take my heart; detach it from the goods, pleasures, joys and vanities of the earth. With all my heart and above all else, I love You, infinite Good and eternal Happiness.

January 23

"You, therefore, must be perfect, as your heavenly Father is perfect" (Mt. 5:48).

Reflection — *"The souls who walk on the path of perfection seek to attain to a union with God which is always more intimate, always more perfect. And which is the most perfect union with God? It is the union of our will with His."*

Servant of God, Mother Thecla Merlo

Prayer — O Jesus, Way of sanctity, make me Your faithful imitator. Render me perfect as the Father who is in heaven.

January 24

"If someone is devout and obeys [God's] will, he listens to him" (Jn. 9:31).*

Reflection — *"Always desire and pray that the will of God be perfectly fulfilled in you."* Imitation of Christ

Prayer — O God, let me always know exactly what Your will is.

January 25

Feast of the Conversion of St. Paul—"And so...we have not ceased to pray for you, asking that you may be filled with the knowledge of God's will ...to lead a life worthy of the Lord, fully pleasing to him, bearing fruit in every good work and increasing in the knowledge of God" (Col. 1:9-10).

Reflection — *"God rewards our good will when He finds no other deeds to reward."*   St. Augustine

Prayer — O St. Paul the Apostle, faithful disciple of Jesus, pray for me, so that I may know God's will, and strengthen me so that I have courage to do it in all things, as you did.

January 26

"Obedience is required by the supreme dominion the Lord has over us as Creator, Father, Redeemer and Sanctifier. It constitutes the greatest merit.... It is the secret for obtaining a great number of graces."   *James Alberione*

Reflection — *"Always obey willingly, always take all things which are disposed from the hands of God. Do His will well, even when He sends us some sickness. Even then say: God's will be done."*
Servant of God, Mother Thecla Merlo

Prayer — My God and my All! I am Yours, in life, in death and in eternity.

January 27

"Obedience is fulfilled by conformity to the divine will. This divine will is manifested through the commandments, the evangelical counsels, and the dispositions of ecclesiastical and civil superiors. It is also manifested in circumstances and events, such as sicknesses, and the various seasons and changes of weather."   *James Alberione*

Reflection — *"Let us remember that we will be happy and serene if we will always do what the Lord wants, day by day, moment by moment."*

Servant of God, Mother Thecla Merlo

Prayer — Our Father, who art in heaven,
Hallowed be thy name.
Thy kingdom come,
Thy will be done,
    On earth as it is in heaven" (Mt. 6:9-10).

January 28

Mary, with admirable humility, submitted to the rite of purification, even though she was not obliged to do so. At Nazareth, Jesus was obedient to Mary and Joseph: "...[Jesus] came to Nazareth, and was obedient to them" (Lk. 2:51).

Reflection — *"All our sanctity consists in these words: to do the will of God well at every moment of our life."*   St. Vincent de Paul

Prayer — O Lord, You are all powerful! Make me a saint.

January 29

"Mary entrusted herself to God and willingly carried out the divine will. She was always prompt to obey in all things. 'It is God's will': This was the motive that lightened her work and rendered her generous in overcoming all obstacles."

James Alberione

Reflection — *When something difficult faces us in life, let us recall the words of Jesus and the example of His Blessed Mother: "Whoever does the will of my Father in heaven is my brother, and sister, and mother" (Mt. 12:50).*

Prayer — "My Father, if it be possible, let this cup pass from me; nevertheless, not as I will, but as you will" (Mt. 26:39).

January 30

"O Lord, our Lord,
    how glorious is your name over all the earth!
What is man that you should be mindful of him...?
You have made him little less than the angels,
    and crowned him with glory and honor.
O Lord, our Lord,
    how glorious is your name over all the earth!"
    (Ps. 8:2, 5, 6, 10)*

Reflection — *"Come now, you who say, 'Today or tomorrow we will go into such and such a town and spend a year there and trade and get gain'; whereas you do not know about tomorrow. What is your life? For you are a mist that appears for a little time and then vanishes. Instead you ought to say, 'If the Lord wills, we shall live and we shall do this or that' " (Jas. 4:13-15).*

Prayer — Your will be done, O Lord.

January 31

The occasions of merit for our sanctification lie in doing what God wants, not what we want. When we place all our trust in the Lord and give Him our *all*, He will not be outdone in generosity. All will be fulfilled with great calm.

Reflection — *Let us place all our trust in the Lord, remembering that "this is the will of my Father, that every one who sees the Son and believes in him should have eternal life; and I will raise him up at the last day" (Jn. 6:40).*

Prayer — "O Mary, make me live in God, with God and for God."

James Alberione

FEBRUARY
Patience in Suffering

February 1

"Come, all you who pass by the way,
  look and see
whether there is any suffering like my suffering..."
  (Lam. 1:12).*

Patience in our tribulations contains the ingredients for all our perfection (cf. Jas. 1:4).

Reflection — *"And let us not grow weary in well-doing, for in due season we shall reap, if we do not lose heart" (Gal. 6:9).*

Prayer — O Jesus, draw me to You! Behind You, I will walk in the footsteps of Your example (cf. Sg. 1:3-4).

February 2

"So you have sorrow now, but I will see you again and your hearts will rejoice, and no one will take your joy from you" (Jn. 16:22).

Reflection — *"The only thing we will take with us will be the merit we have earned in the fervor of each day by patiently bearing all trials and adversities, while spending all our energy for the Lord. Everything else will be useless to us."*

James Alberione

Prayer — Lord, what does it profit us to enjoy the whole world, but fail to save our soul in the process? (cf. Mt. 16:26)

February 3

"Final perseverance is so great a grace that we cannot merit it of ourselves; we can obtain it only by assiduous prayer."   *St. Alphonsus Liguori*

Reflection — *"We must persevere in prayer with Mary, like the Apostles did; only then will the Holy Spirit sanctify us."*   *Timothy Giaccardo*

Prayer — Jesus, I believe in You! I hope in paradise! I love You with all my heart!

February 4

Jesus does not promise a heaven on earth to those who follow Him. On the contrary, He says: "If any man would come after me, let him deny himself and take up his cross and follow me" (Mk. 8:34). Hence, life is a period of trial, but paradise is an eternal reward.

Reflection — *"If God is for us, who is against us?... In all these things we are more than conquerors through him who loved us"* (Rom. 8:31, 37).

Prayer — "O Mary, faithful Virgin, let me persevere in the love of God and fidelity to Him until death." *St. Alphonsus Liguori*

February 5

"If the virtuous man turns from the path of virtue to do evil...none of his virtuous deeds shall be remembered" (Ez. 18:24).*

"Dismas was saved, for, although he began a wicked life, he ended it well. But what happened to Judas, who began well and then died a miserable death?" *St. Peter Chrysologus*

"...The gate is wide and the way is easy, that leads to destruction, and those who enter by it are many" (Mt. 7:13).

Reflection — *Follow exactly the way prescribed for you by the Lord your God (cf. Dt. 5:33). That means to follow in the footsteps of His divine Son.*

Prayer — Come, O Holy Spirit, come and make me a saint!

February 6

"Take your share of suffering as a good soldier of Christ Jesus. The saying is sure:
If we have died with him, we shall also live with him;
if we endure, we shall also reign with him..." (2 Tm. 2:3, 11-12).

Reflection — *Pray that troubled souls suffer with faith and avoid losing the precious merits of their crosses.*

Prayer — O Mary, I will call on you in every danger, doubt or difficulty. Be my strength in every trial.

February 7

"Having crosses in this life means discovering a treasure; suffering them with faith means to benefit from them and better oneself." *Father Faber*

Reflection — *"If we only knew how precious suffering is, we would all ask to suffer."* St. John Vianney

Prayer — "O Jesus, may Your cross always remain rooted in the core of my heart."   *St. Paul of the Cross*

February 8

"Count it all joy, my brethren, when you meet various trials, for you know that the testing of your faith produces steadfastness.... Blessed is the man who endures trial, for when he has stood the test he will receive the crown of life which God has promised to those who love him" (Jas. 1:2-3, 12).

Reflection — *Let us remember that suffering is the sole way of redemption: "Through many tribulations we must enter the kingdom of God" (Acts 14:22).*

Prayer — "O Lord, let me draw near with perseverance to the throne of grace, that I may obtain mercy and find grace to help me in time of need."   *James Alberione*

February 9

"Blessed be my sufferings because they obtain so much glory for me in heaven." *St. Peter Alcantara*

Jesus suffered the most excruciating torments without uttering the slightest complaint.

Reflection — *"Remember the words that I said to you, 'A servant is not greater than his master.' If they persecuted me, they will persecute you" (Jn. 15:20).*

Prayer — "O Lord Jesus, I want whatever You want, and I want it because You want it; I want everything just as You want it; I want it as much as You want it."   *Imitation of Christ*

February 10

"To expiate, to make reparation and to immolate oneself daily signifies contributing to the good of the world more than does fulfilling great works: 'Better is the patient spirit than the lofty spirit' " (Eccl. 7:8).*   *James Alberione*

Reflection — *"If when you do right and suffer for it you take it patiently, you have God's approval. For to this you have been called, because Christ also suffered for you, leaving you an example, that you should follow in his steps." (1 Pt. 2:20-21).*

Prayer — Lord, when it is difficult for me to do what is right in Your eyes, help me to remember Your promise: "Blessed are those who are persecuted for righteousness' sake, for theirs is the kingdom of heaven" (Mt. 5:10).

February 11

"The most Blessed Virgin Mary accepted the sufferings connected with the divine maternity. When Simeon predicted that the sword would pierce her soul, Mary did not rebel. She bowed her head. The salvation of souls was at stake; the greater glory of God was to be procured."

James Alberione

Reflection — *"Suffering passes, but the merit of sufferings born with patience remains for all eternity."*   *St. Vincent de Paul*

Prayer — "Remember, O Virgin Mary, the sword of sorrow which Simeon's prophecy inflicted on your heart when he predicted Jesus' death. Inflict the sword of contrition in our hearts."

James Alberione

February 12

"Final perseverance cannot be merited by us; this great gift of perseverance can be merited only by prayer."   *James Alberione*

Reflection — *Final perseverance is the crown of all graces; it is the grace of graces. Let us constantly ask it of God.*

Prayer — O Mary, may I one day be your joy and crown in heaven.

February 13

Our holy Mother was truly the Virgin of perpetual suffering. "Mary's heart was always Christ's heart. Her sufferings were more intense than those of the martyrs. She suffered because she loved Jesus. The intensity of her love caused the intensity of her sorrows."   *James Alberione*

Reflection — *With the Church, we can apply these words of Jeremiah to the Blessed Virgin:*
   "All you who pass this way,
      look and see:
   is any sorrow like the sorrow
      *that afflicts me...?" (Lam. 1:12)***

Prayer — O Mary, teach us, for the love of Jesus, how to bear what does not please us, how to suffer willingly.

February 14

We know that the following of Christ may often entail suffering. In fact, while speaking to Ananias of the great apostle, St. Paul, our Lord said: "...He is a chosen instrument of mine to carry my name before the Gentiles and kings and the sons of Israel; for I will show him how much he must suffer for the sake of my name" (Acts 9:15-16).

Reflection — *St. Paul tells us: "Do not be ashamed of testifying to our Lord...but take your share of suffering for the gospel.... For this gospel I was appointed a preacher and apostle and teacher, and therefore I suffer as I do. But I am not ashamed, for I know whom I have believed, and I am sure that he is able to guard until that Day what has been entrusted to me" (2 Tm. 1:8, 11-12).*

Prayer — O St. Paul the Apostle, obtain for me the grace to be able to say with you at my death: "I have fought the good fight, I have finished the race, I have kept the faith" (2 Tm. 4:7).

February 15

"Expect to meet sometimes with opposition, contempt, mockery. True disciples are not above the Master. Their crosses are like the passion and cross of Christ: a mysterious source of fruitfulness. This paradox of suffering, offered and fruitful, has been confirmed for twenty centuries by the history of the Church."   *Pope John Paul II*

Reflection — *"Jesus is the loving symbol of what our life should be; He will judge us on the conformity of our life with His."*   *St. Thomas*

Prayer — O Lord, in all that befalls me, I adore Your justice and Your mercy.

February 16

"At the outset of His passion, Jesus Himself experienced interior sufferings: 'He...began to be greatly distressed and troubled' (Mk. 14:33). In His goodness God wishes to make us similar to His divine Son, so He permits us to be marked by the same sufferings which distinguished Jesus."

James Alberione

Reflection — *"Thus does God ordain: The more a soul is loved, the more like Jesus it must become. The higher the degree of sanctity to which a soul is called, the more must that soul be distinguished by patience in bearing its crosses."*   *James Alberione*

Prayer — "My Savior, give me the grace to do my tiny share in lightening the burden of Your heavy cross."   *Richard Cardinal Cushing*

February 17

"For here we have no lasting city, but we seek the city which is to come" (Heb. 13:14).

Reflection — *"We need to keep the thought of heaven ever before us.... Instead of thinking, 'There is this...and that...,' let us think, 'There is heaven!'"*
James Alberione

Prayer — O Jesus Truth, enlighten me to travel only and always in charity and with my gaze fixed on heaven, my ultimate destination.

February 18

"He was spurned and avoided by men,
    a man of suffering, accustomed to infirmity...
Yet it was our infirmities that he bore,
    our sufferings that he endured" (Is. 53:3-4).*

"O Man, look at the price your soul is worth; it is worth the blood of a God!"   *St. Augustine*

Reflection — *"Consider how horrible sin is; it drained Christ of every drop of blood. This should help us persevere in doing only good."*   *Bossuet*

Prayer — Grant, O Lord, that I may judge myself now, so that I may appear before Your holy tribunal already judged.

February 19

"Holiness consists in the patient endurance of our crosses, be it sickness, pain or external suffering due to slander or calumny by individuals who continually cross us. This is just what we must bear —with patience and resignation."   *James Alberione*

Reflection — *Let us remember the wise counsel of St. Paul: "Rejoice in your hope, be patient in tribulation, be constant in prayer" (Rom. 12:12).*

Prayer — Lord, help me not to grow weary and lose heart in suffering.

February 20

"Do not be surprised, beloved, that a trial by fire is occurring in your midst. It is a test for you, but it should not catch you off guard. Rejoice, instead, in the measure that you share Christ's sufferings" (1 Pt. 4:12-13).*

Reflection — *"Happy are you when you are insulted for the sake of Christ, for then God's Spirit in its glory has come to rest on you" (1 Pt. 4:14).*

Prayer — O God, in the difficulties and tribulations of life, help me always to confide in Your grace.

February 21

"I know...you are patient and endure hardship for my cause. Moreover, you do not become discouraged" (Rv. 2:2-3).*

"As your models in suffering hardships and in patience, brothers, take the prophets.... You have heard of the steadfastness of Job, and have seen what the Lord, who is compassionate and merciful, did in the end" (Jas. 5:10-11).*

Reflection — *"We serve God by conquering our temptations and by resigning ourselves in suffering."*
James Alberione

Prayer — "My God, I touch my cross to Your cross. Help me to carry it patiently. I am mindful that if anyone will follow You, he must be a cross-bearer."
Richard Cardinal Cushing

February 22

"There, right in the very street, in the office, in the factory, one becomes holy, provided one carries out one's duty competently, for love of God, and joyfully; in such a way that daily work will not become a 'daily tragedy,' but almost 'a daily smile.' "
Cardinal Albino Luciani

Reflection — *"Let us put great intentions even in our slightest actions, and they will multiply our merits by the hundreds."*
James Alberione

Prayer — "O Lord, help me always to pray enough every day to avoid sin and to fulfill my duties."
James Alberione

February 23

"Sorrow is the inseparable companion of every human life, and, if considered in the light of faith, it is a real treasure. Let us not waste it. We all suffer enough to become saints, if only we knew how to suffer for supernatural reasons."
G. Pasquali

Reflection — *Remember that affliction makes for endurance and endurance for tested virtue (cf. Rom. 5:3).*

Prayer — O Heart of Jesus, full of love and sorrow, let me never be disheartened in tribulations. Rather, lift up my heart to You in heaven.

February 24

"Before the time of Christ, the cross was considered a disgrace, but after Jesus died on the cross it became the sign of victory. Now it is placed on mountain tops, church steeples and bell towers, on or near every altar, in fields, and in classrooms as a sign of redemption."

James Alberione

Reflection — *"Like Jesus, and with Him, we will reach Calvary; then we will also go to heaven with Him. If this is the way to glory, then, courage!"*

James Alberione

Prayer — Lord, stretch out Your helping hand, for You alone can strengthen me.

February 25

God will give us constancy and faith in persecution and trial. Endure these as an expression of God's just judgment in order to be found worthy of His kingdom—Is it not for His kingdom that we suffer? (cf. 2 Thes. 1:4-5)

Reflection — *"Because of original sin, suffering is a natural inheritance for fallen man. As long as one prays, he is helped. When he stops praying, he loses strength."*

James Alberione

Prayer — "O Lord, let me weep over my faults, conquer future temptations, correct sinful tendencies and cultivate holy virtues."   *Imitation of Christ*

February 26

"The crown and fulfillment of the apostolate of holy desires, of prayer and of good example is the apostolate of suffering.

"Jesus Christ closed His life with His passion and death. And the saints who walked in His footsteps follow His example."   *James Alberione*

Reflection — *"Suffering is the apostolate which distinguishes the true apostle from the apostle in name only."*   *James Alberione*

Prayer — O Mary, give us victory in our suffering. Bring relief to those who are afflicted.

February 27

"How could I dare to give myself to vain pleasures when my God hung from a scaffold for my sake?"   *Pope St. Leo the Great*

Reflection — *Let us love the crucifix. Jesus said to St. Gertrude: "When you look at the crucifix with love, God looks at you with love."*

Prayer — "Holy Mother, pierce me through, in my heart each wound renew, of my Savior crucified."   *Stabat Mater*

February 28

Who would want to live without suffering at the sight of Jesus on the cross? Who would dare to complain of any little contradiction?

Reflection — *"Suffering is the furnace where the saints went to become inflamed with love of God and neighbor."*   St. Augustine

Prayer — O Jesus, I want to be Yours in life and in eternity.

MARCH
Prayer

March 1

"...[Jesus] went away and prayed for the third time, saying the same words" (Mt. 26:44).

"Father, if you are willing, remove this cup from me; nevertheless not my will, but yours be done" (Lk. 22:42).

Reflection — *Jesus taught us by His example to be persevering in prayer, without ever becoming tired.*

He taught us to pray above all in moments of trial and of temptation.

Prayer — My Jesus, grant that You may always, everywhere, and in all things dispose of me for Your greater glory and that I may always repeat: "Your will be done."

March 2

"Praying is like keeping a faucet open. As long as prayer is turned on, God's grace continues to flow. As soon as the faucet is shut, the water stops flowing. Graces diminish, and the passions become more violent." *James Alberione*

Reflection — *"Certain graces God does not grant to those who merely pray, but He grants them to those who are persevering in prayer."* St. Augustine

Prayer — O Lord, I resolve to love You above all things until death.

March 3

"We are beggars before God and, as we know, beggars never tire of asking." St. Augustine

Reflection — *"God experiences more pleasure in giving us graces than we do in receiving them, but at the same time He delays in granting them to us until we increase in faith through prayer."*

St. John Vianney

Prayer — O Mary, obtain for me a lively, firm and active faith—faith which saves and produces saints.

March 4

Mary was absorbed in prayer at the little cottage in Nazareth when the angel appeared to her.

She spent thirty-three days in Bethlehem, from the Nativity to the Purification, in continual ecstasy with God.

"Mary's life was a continual colloquy with the heavenly Father and with the Holy Spirit, her divine Spouse." St. Francis de Sales

Reflection — *"God not only does not dislike souls who constantly annoy and trouble Him for favors, but He prefers them, and He loads them with graces."* St. Joseph Cafasso

Prayer — O Mary, teach me how to pray with humility, confidence and perseverance.

March 5

"The most sublime form of love for the Divine Master is to become a living lamp before the most Blessed Sacrament." St. Julian Eymard

"The living lamps before the Blessed Sacrament are the guardian angels of humanity."

Father Matthew Crawley-Boevey

The candles in the Church are symbols of living candles, which are loving souls.

If a church is without souls of prayer, the candles serve no purpose; there is always darkness just the same.

Reflection — *"Jesus listened to the Canaanite woman because she persevered in her request; in the same way will He listen to us if we are constant in praying."* St. Irenaeus

"Do you desire to be heard? Ask with perseverance. If what you are asking is beneficial, you will receive it." St. Bernard

Prayer — Lord, grant me the grace to visit You often in the Blessed Sacrament, to understand and actively participate in Holy Mass, to receive Holy Communion often and with the right dispositions.

March 6

During the night in the garden of Gethsemane, Jesus sweat blood; an angel came to comfort Him.

"Gethsemane was prolonged into our Tabernacles; Jesus waits for someone to comfort Him there, too."   *St. Julian Eymard*

"Here on earth we can do nothing more beautiful than to console Jesus. What joys He will give us in reward!"   *St. Julian Eymard*

Reflection — *"If we only knew who Jesus is, we would spend all the free hours of the day in church."*
                                        St. John Vianney

"The greatest regret we will have in heaven will be to have loved the Eucharist so little and to have given It so little of our time."   *St. Julian Eymard*

"The time we spend before Jesus is the time best spent during the day and during our life."
                                        James Alberione

Prayer — I want to belong to Jesus Christ in life, in death, and in eternity. O Jesus, do not let me separate myself from You.

March 7

"In heaven Mary remains always in the presence of her divine Son, praying unceasingly for sinners."   *St. Bede*

Reflection — *"He who asks favors of God without the intercession of Mary is like a bird who tries to fly without wings."*   *St. Antonius*

"Let us ask many graces from God, but let us ask them through Mary; she is the aqueduct by which they descend to us."   St. Bernard

Prayer — O Mother, accept me as your child. Accompany me throughout my life. Assist me daily and especially in the hour of my death.

March 8

"You should be afraid of falling into sin during the day which you have not meditated."

Blessed John Baptist De Rossi

"Meditation is the source of love and of apostolic drive for great and generous actions."

A. Rodriguez

"God reveals Himself to the soul in meditation and draws it to Himself in prayer."   *Father D'Avila*

Reflection — *"Whatever our meditation is, so is our prayer; whatever our prayer is, so is our life."*

St. Teresa of Avila

"...'Remember your last days, and you will never sin' (Sir. 7:36).* Moreover, you will arrive at a high degree of love, whether it is for God or for your neighbor."   *St. Francis de Sales*

Prayer — Lead us not into temptation, O Lord, but deliver us from all evil, past, present, and future.

March 9

Priests are "ambassadors for Christ; it is as though God were appealing through us, and the appeal that we make in Christ's name is: be reconciled to God" (2 Cor. 5:20).**

Reflection — *Always treat priests with the greatest respect, speaking and thinking well of them: "Whoever honors the priest honors Christ; whoever despises him despises Christ."*   St. John Chrysostom

Pray for them, "because it is extremely difficult for them to maintain themselves at the sublime heights in which God has placed them."

Pope Pius XII

Prayer — Lord Jesus, may all men love Your priests, listen to them, and let themselves be guided by them on the paths leading to heaven.

March 10

An angel commanded Joseph to leave Egypt without stopping on the way in Bethlehem, for fear of the new king, who was one of Herod's relatives.

Joseph pursued his difficult journey as far as Nazareth, where he settled down in a poor, little cottage, working as a carpenter.

In that humble, little house of Nazareth, Jesus grew in wisdom, age and grace with prayer, labor, and obedience.

To everyone, the Holy Family is the example of piety and of fidelity to the Law, especially in regard to religious duties.

Reflection — *Jesus warned us to resist temptations: "Watch and pray that you may not enter into temptation" (Mt. 26:41).*

"If temptation causes you to fall into sin, it is a sign that your prayer is either tepid or insufficient."

St. Vincent de Paul

Prayer — My God, I do not know what will happen to me today. I only know that nothing will happen to me that was not foreseen by You and directed to my greater good from all eternity. This is enough for me. Give me Your strength.

March 11

"What all the other saints can do together with you, O Virgin most holy, you can perform alone without their assistance!

"If you refuse, no one will assist us; if you pray, then everyone will come to our aid and pray for us."   *St. Anselm*

Reflection — *"He whom Mary would not help would be praying in vain for the help of other saints."*   *St. Bernard*

Prayer — "Do not forget, O Mother, that what you possess of grace you owe to us sinners, because it was given to you to use for our salvation."

William Poriscience

March 12

"God regards more the love with which a person performs a work than the amount of work he does."   *Imitation of Christ*

Reflection — *"God lives in us; we are the churches of God! Therefore, we ought to remain in continual adoration."*   *Epistle of St. Barnabas*

Prayer — O Jesus Life, live in me, so that I may live in You.

March 13

"I heard and trembled with fear at the sound of the voice that came from my lips. I, man, called God my Father!"   *St. Peter Chrysologus*

Reflection — *"For you did not receive the spirit of slavery to fall back into fear, but you have received the spirit of sonship. When we cry, 'Abba! Father!' it is the Spirit himself bearing witness with our spirit that we are children of God..."* (Rom. 8:15-16).

Prayer — Oh, how wonderful was Your plan, O Lord, in instituting the sacrament of Baptism, in which You make us Your own children!

March 14

God is not merely light; He is the all-knowing. He is not merely strength; He is the all-powerful. He is not merely life; He is the uncreated Being. But above all, He is love and the root of every paternal gift (cf. Jn. 4:3; Eph. 3:15).

"For what great nation is there that has gods so close to it as the Lord, our God, is to us whenever we call upon him? In him we live and move and have our being..." (Dt. 4:7; Acts 17:28).*

Reflection — *Pray that professors and teachers will give truth, not error, to their students.*

Ask for teachers the grace of humility, so that they will not be puffed up over their knowledge.

Ask for them love for prayer and for study, so that they will be both pious and learned.

Ask for them courage in attacking evil, and constancy which is not shaken by failure.

Ask that the grace of God render their efforts and their words efficacious.

Pray "that every teacher become a broadcaster of Christ and transmit His divine teachings."

Pope Pius XI

"Pray that the school will never ruin the consciences of God's little ones."   *Pope Pius XI*

"Woe to those who inquire after the many curious affairs of men and are little curious of the way to serve me!"   *Imitation of Christ*

Prayer — O Lord, let Your name be praised and let Your work be magnified!

March 15

Jesus permitted a dreadful fear of the passion to invade His soul, in order to sustain and comfort tempted souls.

The Archangel Raphael said to Tobias: Because you were acceptable to God, "...I was sent to test your faith..." (Tob. 12:14).**

Reflection — *"My son, if you aspire to serve the Lord, prepare yourself for an ordeal" (Eccl. 2:1).***

"Temptation shows the virtue of the Christian, as the storm proves the ability of the pilot, and the battle, the courage of the soldier."   *St. Basil*

Prayer — Beloved Father, I am in Your hands. You know what is needed for my progress. Deal with me according to Your good pleasure.

March 16

"God is faithful, and he will not let you be tempted beyond your strength..." (1 Cor. 10:13).

"Blessed be the temptations that permit me to prove to my God how much I love Him!"

St. Teresa of Avila

"To be greatly tempted is a sign that God is calling us to great sanctity and preparing beautiful graces for us."   *Father Lagrange*

Reflection — *"Conquering a strong temptation gives more glory to God than many prayers and fastings."*   *St. Francis de Sales*

Prayer — O Lord, help me to always remain faithful to You: in time of consolation and in time of temptation.

March 17

"If the world does not fall into ruin, it is because legions of souls in hiding immolate themselves for God continually."   *Pope Pius X*

"He who suffers for the salvation of the world is more than a hero; he is a martyr."   *Father Faber*

"The real vocation of religious souls is to be little victims with Jesus." It is not only the vocation of the religious but also of every loving soul.

Timothy Giaccardo

"Many souls go to hell because there is no one to pray and offer sacrifices for them."

The Blessed Mother to the children of Fatima

Reflection — *"Do penance for sinners! I can no longer hold back the angry arm of God from punishing them."*

The Blessed Mother to the children of La Salette

Remember the words of St. Augustine: "If you have saved one soul through your sacrifices, you have predestined your own."

Prayer — O Jesus Life, may my presence bring grace and consolation everywhere.

March 18

"In our creation, redemption and sanctification, God's ultimate purpose is His eternal glory. We are created, redeemed and sanctified to glorify God in this life and in eternity."   *James Alberione*

Reflection — *"The devout soul feels the need to be with God, so that he willingly goes to pray, even if aware that he will have to fight sleepiness, distractions, or temptations all the while."*   *James Alberione*

Prayer — "As a doe longs
  for running streams,
so longs my soul
  for you, my God" (Ps. 42:1).* *

March 19

"Intimate union with Jesus is attained in the Holy Spirit. He infuses His gifts of wisdom, understanding, counsel, fortitude, knowledge, piety, and fear of the Lord."   *James Alberione*

Reflection — *"The Holy Spirit desires to work in all souls, but He is especially active in those souls who leave Him free to act in them, who are docile to the infusion of grace, to the light they receive and to the will of God, and who are united to Jesus in devotion and in prayer life."*   *James Alberione*

Prayer — "Come, Holy Spirit, Creator, come,
From Your bright heavenly throne;
Come, take possession of our souls,
And make them all Your own."   *Veni, Creator Spiritus*

March 20

The first degree of love of God is *vocal* prayer, "which teaches us how to speak with Him."

St. Teresa of Avila

The second degree is *mental* prayer, "which makes us contemplate His perfections."

St. Teresa of Avila

The third degree is *affective* prayer, "which is prayer more of one's heart than of the mind, wherein the affections of the will dominate the reasoning of the intellect."   *St. Teresa of Avila*

The fourth degree is the prayer of *simplicity*, "which consists in a simple, loving gaze upon or loving attention to God Himself or some perfection of His, or to Christ or one of His mysteries."

James Alberione

The fifth degree, *infused recollection*, "is an illumination of the mind. The soul is taken up and conquered by the light coming from God, a light which absorbs its intellectual powers. The Holy Spirit infuses the operations of the gifts of wisdom, understanding, knowledge and, if we wish, counsel, too."   *James Alberione*

The sixth degree is prayer of *quiet*, "in which the soul feels the presence of God and is lost within it, inebriated with love, revelling in the joy that no longer is anything lacking to her."

St. Teresa of Avila

"The last three degrees of prayer are the highest: *prayer of simple union, prayer of ecstatic union,* and *prayer of transforming union.* In this last degree, the person can repeat with St. Paul: 'It is no longer I who live, but Christ who lives in me.'"

James Alberione

Reflection — *Life seems too short for the climbing to the top of this mystic ladder, but each of us has the grace to reach it. So let us try!*

Each one will remain rooted for all eternity at the degree of prayer in which death has overtaken him.

Prayer — To You, O life-giving Spirit, I consecrate my heart. Guard and increase the divine life in me. Grant me the gift of piety. Amen.

March 21

"The saints became saints first of all through meditation; from meditation they drew light, strength, generosity for performing good."

A. Rodriguez

Reflection — *It is by meditating the eternal realities that we learn to be good amid passing reality. What strength the thought of heaven gives to souls!*

Prayer — Virgin Mary, Mother of Jesus, make us saints!

March 22

Jesus communicates grace to us above all through the Eucharistic Sacrifice (Mass) and the sacraments.

"In Mass, Holy Communion and Eucharistic adoration, many come to understand the soul and heart of Jesus. They feel drawn directly to Jesus."

James Alberione

Reflection — *"Let us make ours a Eucharistic day. Let the entire day and all its activities be sustained by the Holy Eucharist."*   *James Alberione*

Prayer — Jesus Master, I will pay special attention to my participation in the Mass and reception of Holy Communion, and to adoration of the Blessed Sacrament, so that You may live in me.

March 23

"For whoever would save his life will lose it; and whoever loses his life for my sake, he will save it" (Lk. 9:24).

Reflection — *"Is our love of Jesus Christ so strong as to cause us to do what He wants, to go where He wills, to say what is pleasing to Him, and to desire Him alone?"*   *James Alberione*

Prayer — Lord, grant me the grace of detaching my heart more and more from all vanity and sinful satisfaction, to seek You only, my supreme and eternal Happiness.

March 24

"The Holy Spirit renders the soul capable of working supernaturally, because He gives it the principle of new life, that is, grace, and brings about the spiritual rebirth of the soul."

James Alberione

Reflection — *"Unless one is born of water and the Spirit, he cannot enter the kingdom of God" (Jn. 3:5).*

Prayer — O Holy Spirit,
Guide our minds with your blest light,
With love our hearts inflame.
And with Your strength, which ne'er decays,
Confirm our mortal frame.   *Veni, Creator Spiritus*

March 25

"After the sacrifice of the Mass and martyrdom, religious life is the most heroic sacrifice that one can make."   *James Alberione*

Reflection — *"The special work, the all-important duty of a religious is this: He must work for his own sanctification."*   James Alberione

Prayer — O God, obtain for us the grace to accept the infirmities, afflictions, and misfortunes of the present life as favors of the divine mercy, so that the vicissitudes of this our exile may not make us grow cold in the service of God, but may make us ever more faithful and more fervent. Amen.

March 26

"In consecrating one's whole heart to God, one must discipline himself by a mortified way of life."
      James Alberione

Reflection — *"Discipline by mortification purifies thoughts and controls the imagination; it also lessens worldly attractions and sanctifies hearts."*
      James Alberione

Prayer — O Jesus, impress on me the virtues of Your most holy heart.

March 27

"The religious vocation is God's call to a more perfect state in community life, with the observance of three vows: chastity, poverty, and obedience."
James Alberione

Reflection — *"To recognize clearly the will of God, it becomes necessary to pray often. The Lord will not fail to reveal His will to a soul who sincerely asks Him."*
James Alberione

Prayer — O Mary, Mother, Teacher and Queen, multiply priestly vocations and fill the earth with religious houses which will be houses of light and warmth for the world, of safety in stormy nights, sources of true piety, and defense against the wrath of God.

March 28

"Prayer, which is the breath of the soul, is a foremost requirement to live common life. It is necessary for the maintenance of grace and for growth in the love of Jesus."
James Alberione

Reflection — *"Prayer is necessary so that the life of Jesus may penetrate us more and more; but, above all, it is necessary in order to avoid discouragement, which does so much harm to the soul."*
James Alberione

Prayer — O Immaculate Virgin, crush the head of that insidious demon of discouragement.

March 29

"...We do not know how to pray as we ought, but the Spirit himself intercedes for us with sighs too deep for words" (Rom. 8:26).

"No one can say 'Jesus is Lord' except by the Holy Spirit" (1 Cor. 12:3).

"For all who are led by the Spirit of God, are sons of God" (Rom. 8:14).

"Do not grieve the Holy Spirit of God" (with venial sin) (Eph. 4:30).

"Do not quench the Spirit" (through mortal sin) (1 Thes. 5:19).

Reflection — *The Holy Spirit is the Consoler and Sanctifier of souls. Let us remain closely united to Him if we truly desire to become saints.*

Prayer — "Come, Holy Spirit,
Giver of graces, Light to hearts!
Come, O heavenly Consoler, our sweet Guest, our refreshment!
Bestow on us Your seven gifts; grant us salvation and eternal joy."   *Veni, Creator Spiritus*

March 30

Jesus loved mankind with an infinite love and offered Himself to the Father for us. God the Father accepted His sacrifice. "With His cross, a new chapter began for everything on earth."
St. John Climacus

And many souls are lost just the same! "Sinners trample on the blood of Jesus and render His sacrifice useless!"   *St. Jerome*

Reflection — *"If Jesus willed to open His side in order to give you His Heart, it is only right that you give Him yours."*   *Blessed Raymond Giardano*

Prayer — "Sacred Heart of Jesus, our peace and reconciliation, have mercy on us!"

Litany to the Sacred Heart

March 31

"They ought always to pray and not lose heart" (Lk. 18:1).

"He who prays saves himself."

St. Alphonsus Liguori

Reflection — *"The only ambition of one who begins to pray must be to make every effort to conform his will to that of God."*   *St. Teresa of Avila*

Prayer — O Jesus, increase our faith, so that we may attain to the eternal vision in heaven.

APRIL
Love of God

April 1

"You shall love the Lord your God with all your heart, and with all your soul, and with all your mind, and with all your strength" (Mk. 12:30; cf. Dt. 6:5).

"What is the measure of love we owe to God? It is to love Him without measure." *St. Bernard*

Reflection — *"Jesus commanded us to love Him with our whole mind, with our whole heart, and with all our strength, and He gives us the grace to do it. Whoever fails to reach this goal has not lived his life entirely."* St. Francis de Sales

Prayer — My God, may I always love You, and may the only reward of my love be to love You even more.

April 2

"For this is the love of God, that we keep his commandments. And his commandments are not burdensome" (1 Jn. 5:3).

"He who has my commandments and keeps them, he it is who loves me; and he who loves me will be loved by my Father, and I will love him..." (Jn. 14:21).

Reflection — *"Let your thoughts seek the truth and your affections, the love of God. Thus serve God whose will it is that we become saints."*   St. Bernard

Prayer — "Let the words of my mouth and the thought of my heart
find favor before you,
O Lord" (Ps. 19:15).*

April 3

"The summit of love for God is to immolate oneself for the sins of humanity."   Father Libermann

"Loving souls do not permit Jesus to go to Calvary by Himself, but they go with Him."

St. John of the Cross

Reflection — *"The souls whose lives are most conformed to Christ are those who sacrifice themselves with Him for the redemption of the world."*

Father Faber

Prayer — May all hearts love You, Jesus Life!

April 4

"Love lifts the soul, and the soul that is lifted to God lifts the world."   Elizabeth Leseur

Reflection — *We should adore Jesus as the King of love. "Who would not love in return a Lover as great as He?"*

St. Augustine

What more could He have done for us than He has done?

Prayer — O Jesus, my Life, my Joy and Source of all good, I love You.

April 5

"The kingdom of God is the kingdom of love. Those who love possess His kingdom within them; those who lack love do not belong to it, and God reigns not in them."   *St. Augustine*

"At the end of our earthly life we will be judged on the greatness of our love."

St. Theresa of Lisieux

Reflection — *"Do you wish to perform marvels in this life? Then grow steadily in grace, and you will be of eternal wonder to everyone in heaven!" J. Scheeben*

Prayer — My God, above all, I ask of You that I may love You more and more.

April 6

"The degrees of love give the degrees of grace; the degrees of grace will give us the degrees of heavenly glory."   *J. Scheeben*

"There is much greater difference between a drop of divine grace and all the goods of this earth than there is between the immensity of the skies and a grain of sand."   *J. Scheeben*

Reflection — *"If you could only visualize the beauty of a soul in the grace of God, you would be ready to die a thousand times rather than lose His grace."*   *St. Brigid*

Prayer — O Jesus, grant me the wisdom to put first in my life the values which are useful and necessary to make me grow closer to You and fill me with your grace.

April 7

The Spirit of Jesus Christ, the Divine Master, is the Spirit of love towards the Father—a fire that purifies, inflames hearts with fervor, sanctifies souls.   *James Alberione*

Reflection — *"How ardently should we burn with love after so many years that the infinite Love has lived in us by means of grace!"*

M. Margaret Claret de La Touche

Prayer — To You, Holy Spirit, I offer, give and consecrate myself as a "living temple" to be consecrated and sanctified.

April 8

"How many souls are not aware that living in the grace of God means to have within themselves the Holy Spirit, Spirit of love!"   *Msgr. D'Hulst*

He is "the living source of grace"; He is "fire"; He is "love"; He is "spiritual anointing."

Reflection — *"Live in the Spirit that is within you; love Him, converse with Him; He will inflame you with love."*   *Cardinal P. DeBerulle*

Prayer — Come, O divine Spirit, and enkindle charity in our hearts!

April 9

"The fruit of the Spirit is love, joy, peace, patience, kindness, goodness, faithfulness, gentleness, self-control..." (Gal. 5:22-23).

"If our love is frugal, it is because we are deaf to the inspirations of the Holy Spirit within us."
M. Margaret Claret de La Touche

Reflection — *"We are made divine because the Holy Spirit lives within us."*   J. Loewengard

"Contemplate Him in the depths of your heart; reflect on who God is, and you will feel happy, and you will live in great fervor."

Christ to St. Catherine of Siena

Prayer — O Lord, let my heart keep vigil near You, even when I am sleeping (cf. Sg. 5:2).

April 10

"Whoever loves God never ceases to think of Him, to desire Him, to speak of Him, and God comes to abide in his soul."   *St. Francis de Sales*

"God flings Himself into the soul who loves Him as a bee flies to suck at the sweetest flower in the garden."   *St. Joseph Cafasso*

Reflection — *"How is it possible to love God without burning with desire to make Him loved? How is it possible to see sin without doing everything in one's power to destroy it?"*   St. John Vianney

Prayer — O my God, You are so great and so holy: I adore You. You have been so offended by me: I ask Your pardon with all my heart.

April 11

"There appeared to them tongues as of fire, distributed and resting on each one of them. And they were all filled with the Holy Spirit" (Acts 2:3-4).

"The Holy Spirit is fire; whoever is filled with the Holy Spirit ought to inflame others."

St. Teresa of Avila

Reflection — *Even we ought to desire, just as the saints did, "to hold in our hands the hearts of all men and to light each one of them with a consuming love for God."*   *St. Teresa of Avila*

Prayer — Grant, O Lord, that I may be the light of the world!

April 12

Grace is like the ticket of our future transfiguration, and the Holy Spirit is the divine stamp we bear in our hearts (cf. 2 Cor. 1:22; Eph. 1:14).

It is a celestial light that rains upon us from the abysses of divinity and floods us with splendor, like dull crystal invested by a divine Sun.

Reflection — *"The bread we beg of God is He Himself who, coming into us by means of grace, transforms us with His deifying nourishment."*

Lacordaire

Prayer — "O Lord, give me Your love and Your grace and I will be rich enough!"   *St. Ignatius Loyola*

April 13

"This has taught us love—that he gave up his life for us" (1 Jn. 3:16).**

"No wood is better able to increase the fire of divine love than the wood of the cross."

St. Ignatius Loyola

Reflection — *"Our life ought to be a prolonged act of love for God, since He has loved us to such an extent!"*   *Msgr. De Segur*

Prayer — "I love You, O Lord, my strength" (Ps. 18:2).*

April 14

"Grace is so great a gift that if only one soul possessed it and the angels had none, they would come from heaven to adore that soul as if he were God."   *J. Scheeben*

Reflection — *"If we could only understand how easy it is to grow in the grace of God with little merits, we would never lose an instant to love God with all our hearts."*   *J. Scheeben*

Prayer — O Jesus Life, grant that I may live eternally in the joy of Your love.

April 15

Vanity of vanities! All things are vanity, except loving God and serving Him alone (cf. Eccl. 1:2).

Imitation of Christ

"Love is a force which no one is able to resist. 'Stern as death is love' (Sg. 8:6)."   *Father Charrier*

Reflection — *"If we could make an act of love every minute of our lives, we would still be doing nothing in comparison to the great love God has for us."*   St. Joseph Cafasso

Prayer — "God is the rock of my heart and my portion forever" (Ps. 73:26).

April 16

"To be without Jesus is a frightening hell; to be with Jesus is a sweet paradise."   *Imitation of Christ*

"If the damned could obtain only one second of time that men waste so thoughtlessly, they would love God with such ardor that they would change from reprobates to saints!"

Words of a possessed to Msgr. Augusto de Sales during an exorcism

Reflection — *"How many more would become saints if they did—to please God—half of what they do to please men."*   St. Thomas Aquinas

Prayer — O Jesus, do not let me separate myself from You.

April 17

"The greatest torment of the damned in hell is their inability to love any longer."   St. Teresa of Avila

"If the damned were able to love God, they would love Him to such a degree that hell would empty in an instant."   St. John Vianney

Reflection — *"To love is the most beautiful, most holy, most precious thing we can possibly do in our lives."*   Msgr. De Segur

Prayer — "A clean heart create for me, O God, and a steadfast spirit renew within me" (Ps. 51:12).*

April 18

Keep your heart free and raised upwards to God, because you have not here a lasting abode. Send heavenward your daily prayers with sighs and tears, that after death your spirit may be worthy to pass happily to our Lord.   *Imitation of Christ*

Reflection — *Our own victories over evil must be the result of love. Love is an elevator that lifts souls to God.*

Prayer — O Jesus Master, establish Your kingdom in us: Your kingdom of truth and of life, of sanctity and of grace, of justice, of love and of peace!

April 19

"God is love, and he who abides in love abides in God, and God abides in him" (1 Jn. 4:16).

Our God is a God of love and peace. Walk in his love! (cf. 2 Cor. 13:11; Eph. 5:2)

Reflection — *"The smallest act of love for God is more useful to the Church than all the other good works together."*   *St. John of the Cross*

Prayer — "To the King of ages, immortal, invisible, the only God, be honor and glory for ever and ever. Amen" (1 Tm. 1:17).

April 20

"Love is light, joy, peace, while sin is darkness and sorrow."   *St. Jerome*

"The resurrection of Jesus was a work of the infinite Love, just as His Incarnation and passion were."   *M. Margaret Claret de La Touche*

Reflection — *Love has infinite radiations: the act of love you now make will still be living before God for thousands of years.*

Prayer — Draw me to Yourself, O Lord. The road is narrow, but it leads to heaven.

April 21

"The Eucharistic Christ is an ardent furnace of charity; let us go to Him to inflame our hearts with His love!

"The tongue on which the Host is placed should not know bitter words, nor the heart in which Jesus dwells know hatred." *Timothy Giaccardo*

Reflection — *"Do you eat of Christ Truth and then lie about your brother? Do you eat of Christ Love and then hate your neighbor?"*   *St. Peter Chrysologus*

Prayer — "Grant us, O Lord, to be always hungry for You, the Food of angels and our daily Bread, full of every delight and sweetness."

St. Bonaventure

April 22

"I have given you an example, that you also should do as I have done" (Jn. 13:15).

"True love rises from the depths of the heart and is nourished with sacrifice."   *St. Vincent de Paul*

Reflection — *"It is sweet and simple to make acts of love for God. Repeat to Him who dwells within you a hundred, even a thousand times a day, 'I love You! I love You!'"*   *Msgr. Carl Gay*

Prayer — Sweet Heart of my Jesus, make me love You more and more.

April 23

"See what love the Father has given us, that we should be called children of God" (1 Jn. 3:1).

"With age-old love I have loved you; so I have kept my mercy toward you" (Jer. 31:3).*

Reflection — *"One who loves sees God within himself and around himself continually."*
Timothy Giaccardo

Prayer — O my God, pardon me for my ingratitude and reservations. I now give myself wholly to You. Take full possession of me and never permit me to retract my offer.

April 24

"The Lord, your God..., is a jealous God" (Dt. 6:15).* He wants our whole heart.

May he never be obliged to complain about us with those words of the Scripture: "This people ...honors me with their lips alone, though their hearts are far from me" (Is. 29:13).*

Reflection — *"Do not open your heart to anyone; take heed to be familiar only with God and the angels."*   Imitation of Christ

Prayer — "Our hearts are made for You, O Lord, and are restless till they rest in You!"   St. Augustine

April 25

To what great heroism did charity move the members of the Holy Family! From their love for God sprang a sublime mutual harmony.

What tragedies strike families without charity! Indeed, "the bonds of charity bind the family closely together; disputes break these ties."

Pope Pius XII

Reflection — *There are persons who suffer continual martyrdom in certain families where the love of God is absent.*

Prayer — Give me strength, O Lord, in bearing my cross. Grant me the virtues of patience and pardon.

April 26

"I will hear what God proclaims
    ...for he proclaims peace" (Ps. 85:9).*

"If God did not annihilate the human race after Adam's great sin, it was because of His extraordinary love for Mary."   St. Bernardine of Siena

Reflection — *Let us love Mary and she will give us a "new garment" as Rebecca gave Jacob, and she will obtain for us the blessings of God the Father.*

Prayer — "O Mary, you are the most beautiful, the most august, the most amiable creature I can possibly think of!"   *St. Leonard of Port Maurice*

April 27

Our Lord repeats to us what He said to the Hebrew people: "Is your heart true to mine, as my heart is to yours?" (2 Kgs. 10:15)**

God loves every soul in proportion to its holiness. How greatly He loved Mary, then, whose initial sanctity was superior to the final sanctity of all the saints!

Reflection — *Man becomes what he loves. "If he loves earth, he becomes earth; if he loves God, he becomes God."*   *St. Augustine*

Prayer — O Mary, be my salvation; I know that those who love you greatly will be holy and will participate one day in your triumph in heaven.

April 28

"Mary, who was born the holiest of holiest, grew remarkably in sanctity from grace to grace until she reached the perfect image of Christ."
    Father William Chaminade

"God contemplated Himself in her, as if in a shining fountain of sublime beauty, and He was pleased."   *St. John Damascene*

Reflection — *"He who loves Mary becomes her son, that is, another Jesus."*   *St. Augustine*

Prayer — My soul and my entire being praise you, O Mary.

April 29

"Mary was so greatly loved by God that He poured into her, at birth, more graces than all the angels and saints had together."   *Suarez*

"She was so holy that a greater sanctity than hers is unimaginable outside of God. God alone is able to understand her sanctity."   *Pope Pius IX*

Reflection — *"If a hundred tongues and a hundred throats would sing, and if I had a thundering voice, I still could not say anything worthy of you, O Mary!"*
St. Bernard

Prayer — "Among so many women who are daughters of sin, only you are a daughter of life, O Mary!"   *Dionysius, Bishop of Alexandria*

April 30

"Mary is mysteriously related to the Holy Trinity, and the three divine Persons have an ineffable tenderness for her."   *Pope Pius XII*

"Our Lord held forth His hand and by His merits preserved the chosen creature, whom by her motherhood He had united so closely to Himself, from the slightest spot of sin which could displease Him, or even for a brief moment disfigure her soul in His most holy sight."

Vassall Phillips

Reflection — *"If God grants a soul an ardent love for Mary, it is a sign that He wants to possess it quickly and perform great works in that soul."*

St. Louis de Montfort

Prayer — I am all Yours, and all that I possess I offer to You my lovable Jesus, through Mary, Your most holy Mother.

MAY
Virtues of Mary

May 1

To Mary we owe the cult of hyperdulia, that is, a very exceptional veneration.

"How can we fail to honor exceedingly her from whom all graces come to us?"   *St. Bonaventure*

"Mary is the plenipotentiary of God for all creatures, heavenly and earthly."   *Pope Benedict XV*

"Mary is so tender that she cannot bear to see anyone around her unhappy."   *Lud. Blosia*

Reflection — *"Know your Mother! Love your Mother! Imitate your Mother! Make your Mother known!"*   *James Alberione*

Prayer — "O Jesus, when the hour comes for my soul to leave my body, let me attain the palm of victory through Mary!"   *Stabat Mater*

May 2

"What Jesus meant when He said, 'Behold your mother,' was this: My wounds are sources of graces, which flow only through Mary."   *St. Andrea*

"Toward you, O Mary, do we poor children of Eve cry; if we do not cry ourselves, our misery cries out for us, because even misery has its own voice."   *Richard of St. Victor*

Reflection — *Let us sincerely consecrate ourselves to Mary, and we will quickly notice that all good things come together with her (cf. Wis. 7:11).*

Prayer — "O Lord, I thank You for having created the Blessed Mother, for having made her so beautiful and for having given her to us as our Mother."

St. Leonard of Port Maurice

May 3

"Mary loves those who love her; she even serves those who serve her."

Blessed Raymond Giardano

"Our Lord created Mary as a lofty bridge by means of which we, running over the waves of the sea, arrive at the port of salvation."

St. James, a Greek monk

How many souls would be in hell for all eternity if Mary had not interceded before God for them!

Reflection — *"When we feel threatening waves rising against us, let us not forget to cry at once: 'Lady, save us! We are perishing!' "*   *Richard of St. Victor*

Prayer — O sweetest Mother, Throne of God and Church of our souls, pray to Jesus that I may find mercy on the day of judgment.

May 4

"Because she is so exalted, is it possible perhaps for her to forget us? It does not suit one so great in mercy to forget such great misery!"

St. Peter Damian

"Wherever there is a misery to alleviate, Mary's mercy runs to aid it!"   *Richard of St. Victor*

"Robbers assail us at night, but when dawn comes they flee; thus flees the devil at Mary's arrival."   *St. Bonaventure*

Reflection — *"Great was Mary's mercy toward the poor and miserable while she was on earth, but it is much greater now that she is in heaven!"*

St. Bonaventure

Prayer — O Queen of Mercy, will you refuse to beg your most holy Son for your most wretched son?... Your Son, Redeemer, for the son redeemed?

May 5

Mary undertook the tedious journey from Nazareth to Hebron, about eighty miles away, to visit her cousin Elizabeth.

Inspired by God, Elizabeth greeted Mary for the first time with the sweet name, "Mother of God" (cf. Lk. 1:43).

Mary expressed her joy in the beautiful canticle, the Magnificat, the most sublime hymn of love and praise that a creature has ever composed.

Humbly and lovingly, Mary remained with Elizabeth for three months, to assist her in her needs. Then she returned to the poor little cottage in Nazareth where she awaited the birth of the Savior, meditating and praying.

Reflection — *We ought to perform all our actions through Mary, with Mary, in Mary, in order to perform them better through Jesus, with Jesus, in Jesus."*   *St. Louis de Montfort*

Prayer — "O fortunate Virgin, only you were worthy to be called by God, 'Daughter,' 'Spouse,' and 'Mother'!"   *St. Augustine*

May 6

A lover of Mary must be pure: "The immaculate One does not bestow her favors on impure or sensual souls."   *Canon Silvio Gallotti*

He ought to be docile: "The humble Handmaid of God seeks souls who are docile and forgetful of themselves."   *Father William Chaminade*

He must be pious: "Mary lived in continual prayer; her devotee must pray and pray continually."   *St. Louis de Montfort*

He must be mortified: "One who loves Mary must silence within himself the desires of the senses and the greedy cravings of the passions."
                              St. John Eudes

He must be recollected: "Every devotee of Mary lives in continual interior solitude, even in the midst of the most distracting occupations."
                              Silvano Giraud

He must be charitable: "Mary, that sweet Mother, loves more the children who better radiate her love."   *St. John Eudes*

He must be humble: "Like God, the Blessed Mother also spurns the proud and gives graces to the humble."   *St. John Eudes*

He must be sincere: "Mary hates any deceit, hypocrisy or lying; anyone who loves her must be a mirror of truth."   *Father William Chaminade*

Reflection — *"Let us imitate Mary most holy. We shall thus find the practice of virtue much easier."*
James Alberione

Prayer — O Mary, be my salvation. I feel my passions, the devil, the world. O Mary, hold me close to you and to your Jesus! Do not permit me to fall, O Mother.

May 7

Mary is always good to us, entirely good and only good to us; her goodness is unchanging.

"In heaven she is all eyes to our miseries and all heart to assist them."   *St. Epiphanius*

From heaven she constantly bends over her children and embraces them warmly.... In fact, we could call her arms the extended arms of love!

Her maternal gaze accompanies us everywhere; it is a gaze full of tenderness for the just, full of sadness for sinners.

Reflection — *The world needs another Pentecost. It is necessary that even the new apostles seclude themselves in the Cenacle with Mary!*

Prayer — Queen of Apostles, pray for us!

May 8

"All graces pass from God to Jesus, from Jesus to Mary, and from Mary to us!"   *St. Bernardine*

"In Mary's hands were deposited all the treasures of divine mercies."   *Pope Leo XIII*

"The grace of God, cure for our ills, comes to us through Mary, like water through an aqueduct."   *St. Bonaventure*

Reflection — *"If you do not want a refusal, entrust to Mary's care everything that you want to offer to God."*   *St. Bernard*

Prayer — To you, O Mary, I consecrate my entire life. Pray for me now and at the hour of my death; and do not leave me until I may prostrate myself before your throne in heaven.

May 9

Mary is the enemy of Satan, who has had a dread fear of her since the day he first saw her from afar in the earthly paradise.

"Mary is so powerful against the devil that he fears a single breath of hers more than all the prayers of the saints."   *St. Louis de Montfort*

What joy the devil experiences when he succeeds in detaching a soul from Mary by contaminating it with mortal sin!

And what joy Mary feels when she succeeds in snatching a sinner from danger and setting him on the road to great sanctity!

Reflection — *"Just as breath gives life to the body, invoking Mary often gives life to the soul."*

St. Germanus

Prayer — O Mary, conceived without sin, pray for us who have recourse to you!

May 10

"God grants us graces according to the office for which we are destined. Because Mary was to become His Mother, He gave her an immeasurable grace."
St. Thomas Aquinas

"The measure for understanding Mary's grace is her dignity as Mother of God, which is an infinite dignity."
Benedict Fernandez

Mary possesses the fullness of grace because God made her a treasury in which He placed all His possessions to be distributed to men."
Richard of St. Lawrence

To her was granted grace greater than that conferred upon all others, "that she might vanquish sin in every respect."
St. Augustine

Reflection — *"We owe Mary a deep love, for she gave us Jesus who is all our strength and all our love."*
James Alberione

Prayer — Receive me, O Mary, Mother, Teacher and Queen, among those whom you love, nourish, sanctify and guide, in the school of Jesus Christ the Divine Master.

May 11

Until the end of the world will occur the same incident that took place in the Cenacle: The Holy Spirit will descend wherever He finds Mary.

"Because of her fidelity to God, Mary obtained a type of jurisdiction over all the communications of the Holy Spirit."   *St. Bernardine of Siena*

"The Holy Spirit, upon entering a soul and finding there Mary, His beloved Spouse, communicates His life to that soul and fills it with gifts."
                                   St. Louis de Montfort

"The fullness of grace is in Christ as the Head from which it proceeds, and in Mary as the Neck through which it passes to the entire body."
                                                     Contenson

"God, seeing us unworthy of receiving graces directly from Him, gave them to Mary so that we receive from her everything He wants to give us."
                                                   St. Bernard

Reflection — *Devotion to Mary is a guarantee of one's correspondence to graces for "he stores up riches who reveres his mother."*

Prayer — "O Mary, you are full of grace! But what am I saying? You have grace in superabundance, and every soul lives of this superabundance communicated to the world."   *St. Bonaventure*

May 12

"Mary is the bud that appeared on the root of Jesse, from which a divine Flower blossomed: Jesus the Savior.

"If you desire to enjoy the fragrance of this Flower, seek to bend with your prayers the stem that bore It."   *St. Bonaventure*

"O Mary, God established you as the Queen of mercy; hence I who am the most miserable of sinners ought to be received by you as a very dear subject."
St. Bernard

"Whoever does not have a great love for the Mother of God cannot have a great love for her Son."
St. Joseph Cafasso

Reflection — *"Invoking Mary frequently showers us with an abundance of graces in this life and an abundance of glory in eternity."*
Blessed Raymond Giardano

Prayer — Gather us 'round you, O our Mother, and pray the Lord of the harvest to send good laborers into His vineyard.

May 13

"Overcome with immense love for us, in order to have us as her children, Mary voluntarily offered Jesus to divine Justice for our salvation."
Pope Leo XIII

As Abraham with a frenzied soul climbed the mountain Moria, for thirty years, so did Mary with her heart torn with sorrow move toward Calvary.

"There were not two sacrifices on Calvary; Jesus and Mary offered the same holocaust with the same heart full of love."
Arnaldo Carnot

Reflection — *"Let us pray to the Blessed Virgin so that she will intercede for us to the Lord; God is much more honored by Mary's petitions than by ours."*
James Alberione

Prayer — Live in our midst, O Mary; blessed are they who dwell in your house.

May 14

Jesus is the Table of the New Law, and it is Mary who teaches us to read it and to observe the laws.

"Mary is the divine Page on which God the Father wrote the Word of God, His Son."

St. Albert the Great

Let us draw near to her and read her!

"She is the living volume of God and of the Word in which, without letters or words, we can read the writer, God, and His Word."   *St. Germanus*

The knowledge of Mary is that limitless field for our studies, for our researches, for our contemplations!

Reflection — *"Do you want to know God? Read Mary as you would a book; look at her as you would a mirror; reflect on her as you would a picture."*
George de Rhodes

Prayer — "In you, O most holy Lady, have I placed my trust; do not let me be confounded in eternity!"
St. Bonaventure

May 15

"Love, if it does not find souls similar to itself, renders them similar to it."   *M. T. Cicerone*

Whoever loves Mary must seek to become similar to her.

Our life ought to be a continual gaze upon Mary, in order to conform our conduct to her examples.

"When will it happen that souls will inhale Mary as bodies the air? At that time she will accomplish marvelous works in them."

St. Louis de Montfort

Reflection — *"Live in Mary's heart, love what she loves, desire what she desires, and you will have peace, joy, and sanctity."* St. John Eudes

Prayer — O Mary, I consecrate myself to you and through you to Jesus.

May 16

Every devotee of Mary performs everything under her gaze. Brief remembrances, tiny aspirations sent in flight, fleeting glances at her images are testimonials of love that he gives her continually. Alone or in the company of others, along the street or in his room, he is always murmuring some ejaculation to her. In doubts and struggles, in pains and joys, the Hail Mary passes from his lips to the heart of the Virgin and flows back to him in waves of graces.

Reflection — *O Mary, it is sweet to turn my first look upon you in the morning, to walk beneath your mantle during the day, to fall asleep under your gaze at night.*

Give me a penitent life so that I may have a holy death and may one day raise my voice with those of the saints, to praise you in paradise!

Prayer — When I can no longer call on you, O Mary, then take possession of me and offer to God the last and most ardent act of love of my life—an act which will become eternal in paradise.

May 17

"No one can acquire an intimate union with Jesus and a perfect fidelity to the Holy Spirit without being greatly united to Mary."

St. Louis de Montfort

"We will never reach the fullness of love until Mary will be for us as much as she was for Jesus."

Father William Chaminade

"It was never written of anyone that he became a saint without having a special devotion to Mary."   *St. Bonaventure*

Reflection — *When something goes wrong for us, let us rejoice at the thought that Mary's gaze is always following us and smiling on us!*

Prayer — My Mother, my hope!

May 18

"The *Hail Mary* is the most beautiful compliment we can pay to Mary because God, to conquer her heart, first offered it to her through an angel."

St. Louis de Montfort

"God exalted Mary like a palm, to tell us that he who entrusts himself to her is certain of victory."

St. Albert the Great

"The *Hail Mary* is a heavenly dew which sprinkles the dry and sterile soul until it bears fruit at an opportune time."   *St. Louis de Montfort*

Reflection — *"Each time we turn our eyes toward Mary, a wave of love passes from her to us."*

Beaudenom

Prayer — Hail Mary, full of grace! The Lord is with you; blessed are you among women, and blessed is the fruit of your womb, Jesus.

May 19

"To the saints God gave holy mothers; He selected for Himself the holiest of all mothers."
Pope Pius XI

Mary, the most perfect of all mothers, is an admirable example to them of every virtue.

"Praying for the sanctity of mothers means to pray for a perfect society."   *Pope Pius XII*

The words of mothers are imprinted indelibly in the hearts of their children. It has been said that a holy mother is worth more than one hundred good teachers.

If a child is bad, his mother can still save him; but who will save the children of a wicked mother?

Through Mary's intercession, let us ask for mothers the virtues of faith, abnegation, patience, humility.

Reflection — *"Mary is the Mother of the Mystical Body and, as such, she never condemns or disrupts it, but reanimates and vivifies all who are presented to her."*   Bossuet

Ask Mary to give your own mother great sanctity and a beautiful paradise.

Prayer — Sweet Heart of Mary, be my salvation.

May 20

Mary is Queen of Apostles because she is the Mother of Jesus, the Apostle of the Father (cf. Jer. 49:14).

She is Queen of Apostles because she "formed them and directed them in their preaching."

St. Cyril of Alexandria

She is Queen of Apostles because "she routed all the heresies."   *St. Cyril of Alexandria*

She is Queen of Apostles because she is Mother of grace and channel of mercy.

Reflection — *"Mary is the echo of God. If we say, 'Mary,' she will answer, 'God.' For this reason, union with her is always followed by union with God."*

St. Louis de Montfort

Prayer — O Mary, "make me prepare for death, fear judgment, avoid hell, and obtain paradise."

Imitation of Christ

May 21

"No true devotee of Mary will be damned, because she is the terrible Conqueror of the devil."

St. Alphonsus Liguori

"Mary is the miraculous vessel which will never become shipwrecked."   *St. Louis de Montfort*

"In heaven Mary most holy will glorify those that glorified her on earth."   *Richard of St. Lawrence*

Reflection — *A true devotion to Mary is a sign of a true devotion to Jesus Christ. God has united Mother and Son; let man not separate them.*   *James Alberione*

Prayer — O powerful Virgin, free me from the snares of Satan and help me to arrive laden with merits at the harbor of salvation!

May 22

"In the passion Mary suffered so horribly that her torments surpassed the sum total of the sorrows of all the martyrs."   *St. Ildefonsus*

"Seated atop Mount Calvary with your dead Son on your knees, O Mary, you became the executor of His will and the distributor of all graces."   *Father Faber*

"I was not born for present things, but for the future; for these eternal things only, let me live, O Mary, and not for those passing."   *St. John Berchmans*

Reflection — *"Let us take refuge in Mary; she is a powerful, merciful, and understanding Mother."*
   James Alberione

Prayer — "Make me weep with you and share the pains of your crucified Son all the days that I live."
   Stabat Mater

May 23

"Come to meet me, O Mary, when my soul leaves this earth, and accompany me to heaven's threshold!"   *St. Bonaventure*

"Console me with the sight of your radiant countenance; be my ladder to heaven's door; obtain for me the grace of everlasting peace and a throne in eternal glory before your Son!"
   St. Germanus

"Whoever dies in Mary's embrace will awake in the embrace of the Lord."   *G. Roschini*

Reflection — *"Blessed are they who follow in Mary's footsteps; blessed are they who constantly and truly aim for perfection; their life will abound in merits."*   *James Alberione*

Prayer — "O sorrowful Virgin, give me strength to accept my little crosses with patience and joy!"
                    St. Bonaventure

May 24

Of what value is it for me to enumerate my merits and victories if I fail to number your favors among them, O Mary?

"Mary is like the universal sacrament under which God loves to hide in order to give Himself to us in a way suitable for our infirmity."
                    Canon Silvio Galotti

"Just as the devil always goes in search for someone to devour, so Mary is always looking for someone she can help in any way."
                    Pope St. Leo the Great

Reflection — *"Let us not seek comfort in creatures; they very often do nothing but increase our sorrow. Let us go to Mary, and we shall always find the merciful Mother who consoles and comforts."*
                    James Alberione

Prayer — Blessed be the name of the great Mother of God, Mary Most Holy!

May 25

"Just as there was never a love like hers, so also there was never a sorrow like hers."

Richard of St. Victor

"From the moment of Jesus' birth, the black shadow of the cross weighed heavily on Mary's heart." *Bossuet*

"She knew that she was raising the most lovable of sons for the most horrible of torments possible to man." *St. Cyriacus*

"Whoever wishes the grace of the divine Spirit must seek the Flower on this stem; by the stem he will reach the Flower, and by the Flower, the Spirit." *St. Bonaventure*

"Through you, O Mary, we have access to the Son, so that He who was given to us through your love will receive us through your love." *St. Bernard*

Reflection — *"With divine grace the apostolate of suffering is possible to everyone. And since everyone has something to suffer, we can change into virtue this inevitable suffering."* James Alberione

Prayer — O Mary, protect us from the attacks of Satan, defend us from the wrath of the Judge, and draw us from the reefs of this sea to the port of happiness!

May 26

"O you who flounder amid the vicissitudes of life, as on the waves of a stormy sea, do not divert your eyes from Mary, Star of the Sea!

"If the winds of temptation blow about you, if your frail bark is hindered by the rocks of tribulations, look to the Star, invoke Mary!

"If you are tossed by the waves of pride or ambition, of slander or envy, look at the Star, invoke Mary!

"If anger or avarice or sensuality rock the tiny vessel of your heart, look at Mary!

"If you are troubled by the enormity of your sins and are on the verge of sliding into the abyss of discouragement, think of Mary!

"In dangers, in afflictions, in critical moments, remember Mary, call upon Mary!"   *St. Bernard*

Reflection — *"Live in Mary with a childlike simplicity that is neither concerned over present things nor those of the future, but abandoned to her protection in everything."*   *St. Bernard*

Prayer — "Into your hands, O Lady, I commend my spirit."   *St. Gabriel of the Sorrowful Mother*

May 27

"Never permit Mary's name to be far from your lips; may the thought of her be always fixed in your heart!

"By following her, you can never go astray; by praying to her you will never fall; by thinking of her you will never err; protected by her, you need not fear; guided by her, you will reach salvation."
    St. Bernard

"If life weighs heavily on your shoulders, if temptation seizes you, you have a safe harbor: the heart of Mary."   *Father William Chaminade*

Reflection — *"How wise is the man who seeks to be in this life the way he wishes to be found at death!"*   *Imitation of Christ*

Prayer — O Mary, "sweet awakener of consciences which have fallen asleep," spur me ever forward and make me reach the sanctity destined for me by God.   *Invocation of Byzantine Liturgy*

May 28

"Mary does not love us in jest but with a startlingly serious love!"   *St. Angela of Foligno*

Therefore, do not forget the tears of your mother! (cf. Sir. 7:27)

Reflection — *Reflect on the thought that years and years before you were born you were already living in Mary's heart; she had already loved you and suffered for you!*

Prayer — Oh Mary, give us piety—beautiful, holy, fruitful piety that is useful for everything (cf. 1 Tm. 4:8).

May 29

"Be favorable to us, O most august Queen, you who were made the all-powerful Mother by your Son!"   *Richard of St. Lawrence*

Take our defenses near His throne. He denies you nothing in heaven because you denied Him nothing on earth!

"And after this our exile, show unto us the blessed fruit of your womb, Jesus. O clement, O loving, O sweet Virgin Mary!"   *Hail, Holy Queen*

Reflection — *"Let us ask ourselves: Is our heart patterned after the heart of Mary? Is it made according to the heart of Jesus Christ? Does it have the same intentions, aims, and aspirations?"*

James Alberione

Prayer — Speak, O Lady, for Your Son is listening to you!... Speak to Him about us sinners!

May 30

"All the grace that flows into the world comes from heaven only through Mary and with her."

St. Lawrence Justinian

"How could she who is the ladder to paradise and gate of heaven for us be without a superabundance of grace?"   *St. Antoninus*

"Many graces, if we ask them of God, we will not obtain; if we ask them of Mary, we will obtain them, not because she is more powerful but because God intends to honor her in this manner."

St. Anselm

Reflection — *"If we wish to find grace, let us turn to Mary. She was the first to find it, and she will always find it for us."*   *Richard of St. Lawrence*

Prayer — "For the wounds of your Son, O Mary, pierce my heart with a wound of love!"

St. Bonaventure

May 31

"The *Hail Mary* is the hammer which crushes the devil and is the joy of the angels, the melody of the predestined, the canticle of the New Testament.

"The *Hail Mary* is a chaste and loving kiss that we give to Mary, a brilliant red rose we offer to her, a precious pearl we present to her.

"It is a divine flower gathered by an archangel in heavenly gardens and shown to us so that we will offer it to Mary." *St. Louis de Montfort*

To have an aversion to the Hail Mary or to be negligent in reciting it is a probable sign of damnation!

"Whoever greets Mary lovingly will be greeted by her, and her greeting is a special grace that she grants every time."

The Blessed Virgin to Blessed Alan de La Roche

If such is the worth of the Hail Mary, let us sow it often and everywhere, and we will gather graces and blessings.

"When a soul on earth recites the Hail Mary well, it renews in my heart the joys of the Incarnation." *The Blessed Mother to St. Gertrude*

Reflection — *"Say the entire rosary well every day; in the hour of death you will bless the moment you chose so holy a resolution."* *St. Louis de Montfort*

Prayer — Hail, O Mary, our Mother, Teacher and Queen.... My soul and my entire being praise you.

JUNE

Love of Neighbor

June 1

"A new commandment I give to you, that you love one another; even as I have loved you, that you also love one another" (Jn. 13:34).

"In the kingdom of Christ, all is based on love; all is love. He desires that everything in our lives will also be based on love."   *St. Francis de Sales*

Reflection — *In an instant, we can love heroically. "And it is so beautiful to love! It will take all eternity to understand the essence of love."*   *St. John Vianney*

Prayer — My God, I love You above all things with all my heart; and for love of You, I love my neighbor as myself!

June 2

Jesus not only advises us to love our enemies; He commands us: "But if you do not forgive men their trespasses, neither will your Father forgive your trespasses" (Mt. 6:15).

"Be kind to one another, tenderhearted, forgiving one another, as God in Christ forgave you" (Eph. 4:32).

Reflection — *Let us reflect on what we say so often: "Forgive us our trespasses as we forgive those who trespass against us."*

Prayer — Jesus, Infinite Goodness, have mercy on us.

June 3

"Blessed are the merciful, for they shall obtain mercy" (Mt. 5:7).

"Be assured that the more you advance in charity toward your neighbor, the more will you progress in the love of God."   *St. Teresa of Avila*

Reflection — *How wonderful it would be to be able to say to Christ at the judgment: "Treat me as I have treated others!"*

Prayer — O God, may my heart love You more and more; may I love my neighbor for love of You.

June 4

"If any one says, 'I love God,' and hates his brother, he is a liar..." (1 Jn. 4:20).

"We do not love God if we do not serve Him, and we do not love our neighbor if we do not help him when he is in need."   *St. Vincent de Paul*

Reflection — *Charity is not self-seeking (cf. 1 Cor. 13:5). In fact, whenever an occasion presents itself, the person of charity willingly sacrifices himself for his neighbor.*

Prayer — O God, who, to communicate Your love to men, sent Your only Son Jesus Christ into the world, impress on me the virtue of fraternal charity.

June 5

Jesus, scarcely able to speak, still found enough strength to tell His enemies that He pardoned them and was praying for them.

He also commands us to pardon others: "...As the Lord has forgiven you, so you also must forgive" (Col. 3:13; cf. Lk. 6:37).

Reflection — *Be kind toward those who have offended you; speak in friendly tones to those toward whom you are least inclined; do a favor for those who have denied you one. Sow goodness and you will reap goodness.*

Prayer — O Jesus Master, Way, Truth and Life, grant me the wisdom, virtue and love which sustained You in Your toil-filled days.

June 6

"God so greatly loves those who pardon others that He bears them securely to great sanctity."
St. Francis de Sales

"Should not you have had mercy on your fellow servant, as I had mercy on you?" (Mt. 18:33)

Reflection — *"All of us have some defects. Let us bear those of the others, and the others will bear ours."*   *Timothy Giaccardo*

Prayer — Mary, refuge of sinners, obtain mercy for me.

June 7

"Love for our neighbor is the surest way to prove our love for God."   *St. Teresa of Avila*

See how Mary forgot her own interests at Nazareth, to go and assist Elizabeth in Hebron.

Reflection — *Just think that Mary, who is so great, takes care of you who are so little! She, as holy as she is, loves you, a sinner, so much! And she loves you more than your angel, even more than yourself!*

Prayer — O holy Virgin, I am yours, entirely yours and always yours, in life and in death, in time and in eternity!

June 8

"Whoever acts as if the love of God consists only in saying 'Lord, Lord,' without renouncing himself, has but the shadow of love."

St. Teresa of Avila

"True love of neighbor is pure, constant, generous, supernatural."   *Timothy Giaccardo*

Reflection — *"Only he who loves God above all things knows how to love his neighbor as himself, for the love of God."*   *St. Vincent de Paul*

Prayer — O Jesus, I, an unworthy sinner, prostrate before You, adore Your Heart, which has so greatly loved men and has not spared anything for them.

June 9

"Blessed are the peacemakers, for they shall be called sons of God" (Mt. 5:9).

"Where there are dissensions there is not Christ, because He is Peace."   *Pope Pius XII*

Reflection — *"In so many families Jesus is scourged by quarrels and crucified by hatreds. Many aged souls weep and many young people are lost because charity does not reign in their families."*

Pope Pius XII

Prayer — O most Sacred Heart of Jesus, protect our families!

June 10

"Do to no one what you yourself dislike" (Tb. 4:15).*

"And as you wish that men would do to you, do so to them" (Lk. 6:31).

Reflection — *"By this all men will know that you are my disciples, if you have love for one another"* (Jn. 13:35).

Prayer — O Lord, may we be of one mind in truth and of one heart in charity.

June 11

"Forgive your neighbor's injustice; then when you pray, your own sins will be forgiven" (Sir. 28:2).*

"Love your enemies and pray for those who persecute you; do good to those who hate you" (Mt. 5:44; Lk. 6:27).

Reflection — *Let us put into practice the wise counsel of St. Paul: "Do not let the sun go down on your anger"* (Eph. 4:26).

Prayer — O divine Holy Spirit, eternal Love of the Father and of the Son, I adore You, I thank You, I love You, and I ask You pardon for all the times I have grieved You in myself and in my neighbor.

June 12

During His three years of public life, Jesus traveled throughout Palestine "...doing good and curing all..." (Acts 10:38).**

Each one of us ought "to show forth the light of Jesus Christ in words and actions, by radiating charity." *St. Julian Eymard*

Reflection — *"He who never sacrifices himself for others cannot say that he loves his neighbor."*

St. Vincent de Paul

Prayer — O Jesus, Divine Master, I thank You for having come down from heaven to free us from so many evils by Your teachings, holiness and death.

June 13

These things delight the Lord:
"Harmony among brethren, friendship among
    neighbors..." (Sir. 25:1).*
"Behold, how good it is, and how pleasant,
    where brethren dwell at one! (Ps. 133:1)*

Reflection — *"Charity that is only on the lips and not in the heart is a mask, not a virtue."*

St. Vincent de Paul

Prayer — Jesus Master, dispose my heart to seek only Your glory and the peace of hearts.

June 14

"Mary loved us so much that she willingly made the sacrifice of her beloved Son in order to save us."   *St. Bonaventure*

"She loved us to such an extent that, if God had willed so, she would have immolated herself for us with her own hands."   *Gerson*

Reflection — *"Every day I desire to grow a little in the love of her who has loved me so much."*

                                                    St. John Berchmans

Prayer — O Mary, be for us the bright moon in the night of exile, the luminous dawn in the morning of eternity, splendid sun on the day of beatific vision!

June 15

"Love never ends;...as for tongues, they will cease; as for knowledge, it will pass away" (1 Cor. 13:8).

Paradise is the blossoming of charity; whoever loves in a greater degree on earth will shine the more brilliantly in heaven.

Reflection — *Oh, if we had only a spark of true charity, how well would we understand that earthly things are all saturated with vanity!*

Prayer — Keep far from us, most loving Father, the plague of error and corruption which contaminates the world.

June 16

"Bear with one another charitably, in complete selflessness, gentleness and patience" (Eph. 4:2).**

"If you cannot bear your neighbor, how will God bear you?"   *St. John Chrysostom*

Reflection — *"If you are unable to conform your own life to the standards you desire, what right have you to expect the others to be the way you want?"*
Imitation of Christ

Prayer — Father, may all people become, through Jesus Christ Your Son, Your children.

June 17

"He who loves his brother abides in the light, and in it there is no cause for stumbling. But he who hates his brother is in the darkness and walks in the darkness..." (1 Jn. 2:10-11).

Reflection — *"Whoever receives Jesus often in Communion must afterwards radiate Him in his own life."*   *St. John Vianney*

Prayer — O Jesus, Exemplar of charity, make me similar to You.

June 18

"Charity is so much more true the less it contains other motives."   *St. Francis de Sales*

"You, therefore, must be perfect, as your heavenly Father is perfect" (Mt. 5:48).

Reflection — *"We often think we have charity when actually we have only natural love because we love persons through sentimentality or our own interests."* Imitation of Christ

Prayer — I love You, O Lord and Way, with all my strength, because You have commanded us to observe Your commandments perfectly.

June 19

"If he sins against you seven times in the day...you must forgive him" (Lk. 17:4).

"Whoever has enemies ought to rejoice; by pardoning them, he will have the means by which God will pardon him of his faults." A. Manzoni

Reflection — *"Whoever promptly pardons an injury thereby heals the wound in his own heart."* St. Vincent de Paul

Prayer — Jesus, Life of hearts, have mercy on us.

June 20

I do not say to pardon him seven times, but seventy times seven (cf. Mt. 18:22).

"For with the judgment you pronounce you will be judged" (Mt. 7:2).

"For judgment is without mercy to one who has shown no mercy..." (Jas. 2:13).

Reflection.— *"Be always ready to pardon; we have so much need to be pardoned ourselves."* St. Teresa of Avila

Prayer — Most Sacred Heart of Jesus, have mercy on us.

June 21

"Carrying Jesus for nine months in her womb, Mary became the living mirror of love for Him."

St. Alphonsus Liguori

"Her heart is so loving that, in comparison to it, the heart of any other mother is a piece of ice."

St. John Vianney

Reflection — *"The sum total of the love of all mothers for their children can never equal the love Mary has for only one soul."*   *St. Alphonsus Liguori*

Prayer — Sweet heart of Mary, be my salvation.

June 22

"The name of Mary is compared to oil because, like oil, it heals wounds, emanates a fragrant perfume, and enkindles a flame."

Blessed Alan de La Roche

"Just as she alone is greater than all the angels and saints together, so is she more solicitous for us than them all."   *St. Augustine*

Reflection — *There is an imperceivable garment of graces, of vigilance, of foresight and providence with which Mary wraps the life of each one of us.*

Prayer — We fly to your protection, O holy Mother of God, despise not our petitions in our necessities, but ever deliver us from all dangers, O glorious and blessed Virgin.

June 23

Charity bears with all things, is not provoked, does not rejoice over wickedness but rejoices with the truth (cf. 1 Cor. 13:5-7).

"True charity excludes sympathies and antipathies and loves everyone in Jesus and for Jesus."

St. Francis de Sales

Reflection — *"An ounce of real love for our neighbor is worth more than a quantity of other virtues."*

St. Francis de Sales

Prayer — Jesus, Model of the saints, have mercy on us.

June 24

"Love is patient and kind..." (1 Cor. 13:4). That means to perform good deeds every time it is possible.

"Nothing is sweeter than love, nothing stronger, nothing more sublime, nothing greater or more beautiful!"   *Imitation of Christ*

Reflection — *"He does much who loves much; he does much who performs his duty well."*

Imitation of Christ

Prayer — Heart of Jesus, burning furnace of charity, have mercy on us.   *Litany of the Sacred Heart*

June 25

"As you did it to one of the least of these my brethren, you did it to me" (Mt. 25:40).

"Respect the others as the pupil of your eye, and I will do the same for you."

Jesus to St. Gertrude

Reflection — *"Love of our neighbor moves us to action, and whatever is done through charity, even if it is little, brings forth much fruit."*

Imitation of Christ

Prayer — "O Lord, make me obey my superiors, assist the sick, help my friends, and pardon my enemies!"   *Imitation of Christ*

June 26

"Do not speak ill of anyone. He who slanders wounds three people: himself, his listener, and the one he speaks of."   *St. Bernard*

"Flee from the malicious. Whoever listens to slander with interest is already a slanderer."

La Rouchefoucauld

Reflection — *"If anyone thinks he is religious, and does not bridle his tongue but deceives his heart, this man's religion is vain" (Jas. 1:26).*

Prayer — Heavenly Father, guard my mind, my heart and my senses, in order that I may know, love and serve only Jesus, and employ all my energies for His glory.

June 27

"So faith, hope, love abide, these three; but the greatest of these is love" (1 Cor. 13:13).

"All our sanctity is a question of love because love contains all the laws" (cf. Mt. 22:40)

St. Francis de Sales

Reflection — *"Let us try to have a good heart that knows how to love as Jesus loved."*   *James Alberione*

Prayer — To You, O life-giving Spirit, I consecrate my heart. Fill it with true love.

June 28

"Examine yourself often on charity in your thoughts and habitually think well of everyone; only then will our Lord be pleased with you."

St. Bernard

"We lose time as well as commit sin when we judge the others; if we examine ourselves instead, we always gain."   *Imitation of Christ*

Reflection — *"Always think well of everyone; that is what gives so much peace to our hearts."*

Timothy Giaccardo

Prayer — O Mary, obtain for me the grace to know, imitate and love ever more the Divine Master.

June 29

"You never make a mistake by thinking well of everyone; but you can be gravely mistaken by thinking evil of even one person."   *Lacordaire*

"If you do not have the duty of judging the others, then always excuse them. Excuse the intention if you cannot excuse the action."

St. Bernard

Reflection — *"Pardon delights the heart and renders it capable of great and generous actions."*

Father Libermann

Prayer — Jesus, I give You all of my heart. Ever keep my eyes on Your ways.

June 30

"When all is said and done, charity towards our neighbor is love of God; it is to love God in our neighbor."

James Alberione

Reflection — *"Never render evil for good, nor evil for evil, but only good for evil."*   Timothy Giaccardo

Prayer — O Jesus Christ, our Master, You are the Way and the Truth, and the Life. Grant that we may learn the supernatural knowledge of Your charity.

JULY

Purity

July 1

Who is she that comes forth as the morning rising, fair as the moon, bright as the sun? Your garment was white as snow and your face, resplendent as the sun.

Reflection — *"A God could have none other than a Virgin for a Mother; and a Virgin could have none other than a God for a Son."* St. Bernard

Prayer — "All glory to you, O Immaculate, to you, O loveliest of all beauties." *George of Nicomedia*

July 2

"A shoot shall sprout from the stump of Jesse, and from his roots a bud shall blossom" (Is. 11:1).*

Reflection — *"Mary is the root from which Christ, the Lily of the valley, sprouted. She is the stem on*

which the divine Flower of salvation, Jesus the Redeemer, blossomed."   St. John Climacus

Prayer — We admire your admirable virginity, uninjured amid the brambles, O Mary!

July 3

"Mary was called the lily among thorns because just the mere sight of her instilled chaste thoughts into everyone."   Dionysius the Carthusian

Reflection — *"I want to keep my eyes pure so that I can better contemplate the beauty of Mary in heaven."*   St. John Berchmans

Prayer — O Mary, I give myself entirely to you; accept me as your property and possession.

July 4

Mary is the Mother of the Word made Flesh. With these very words, Elizabeth greeted her: "And why is this granted me, that the mother of my Lord should come to me?" (Lk. 1:43)

She is the most chaste of all earthly creatures. She introduced herself in this manner to humble Bernadette: "I am the Immaculate Conception."

Reflection — *"You can never think of Mary without her praying to God for you."*

St. Louis de Montfort

"There are only three ways to conquer impurity: fasting, flight from occasions of sin, love for Mary."

St. Robert Bellarmine

Prayer — O Mother, never permit me to succumb to temptation, but teach me to use it as a ladder to climb nearer to you!

July 5

"A horrifying staircase leads to the door of hell; its steps are bad thoughts, delight in evil, consent to sin, the habit of sinning, despair, and final damnation."

St. Bernard

Reflection — *The only real evil in the world is sin, because it closes heaven's door to us, and, "What profit would a man show if he were to gain the whole world and destroy himself in the process?" (Mt. 16:26)**

Prayer — O Lord, may the many tears of Your divine Mother be not in vain for me!

July 6

"In heaven the pure will sing a canticle that only they will know" (cf. Rv. 14:4).

St. Gregory the Great

Reflection — *"At Communion, Jesus asks us to offer Him our hearts as an altar where He can celebrate Mass. Give Him a pure heart, so that the altar may be spotless."*   C. De Condren

Prayer — "Lord, I consecrate my thoughts to You so that they may be from You; my words, that they may be about You; my actions, that they may be according to You; my crosses, that they may be for You."

Imitation of Christ

July 7

"Peace I leave with you; my peace I give to you; ...let not your hearts be troubled" (Jn. 14:27).

"There is a peace that God alone can give and only that peace fills the heart. It is the peace of a pure conscience, of true love, of good will."

St. Teresa of Avila

Reflection — *"We possess true peace when the flesh is subjected to the spirit and the spirit is subjected to God."*   *Pope St. Leo the Great*

Prayer — Heart of Jesus, our Peace and Reconciliation, have mercy on us.   *Litany of the Sacred Heart*

July 8

"Whoever sincerely desires to become a saint must nourish his soul with mortifications of every kind, just as he nourishes his body with bread."

Christ to Sr. Consolata Benigna

Reflection — *Mortification of the senses is the "ABC's" of sanctity.*

Prayer — "O Lord, help me to conquer sensuality with mortification, wrath with meekness, tepidity with fervor."   *Imitation of Christ*

July 9

"Into a soul that plots evil wisdom enters not, nor dwells she in a body under debt of sin" (Wis. 1:4).*

The Holy Spirit warns us: "He who loves danger will perish in it" (Sir. 3:25).*

Reflection — *"What we all lack most is a sense of sin; we do not fear it enough."*   *E. Balfour*

Prayer — From all sin, deliver us, O Lord.

July 10

Purity is a blessed virtue. God loves pure souls and adorns them with treasures of graces. Carefully guard your interior purity because "out of the heart come evil thoughts, murder, adultery, fornication, theft, false witness, slander" (Mt. 15:19).

Reflection — *"When one's heart is impure, I do not merely say that his purity of body is worth little; I say it is worth nothing."*   *St. Ambrose*

Prayer — O Mary, conceived without sin, pray for us who have recourse to you!

July 11

Purity is a life-giving virtue. It strengthens one's will; it refines the character; it conserves health of mind and body. Purity is a generous virtue: "Pure souls know how to become heroes and saints."   *St. Francis de Sales*

Reflection — *"Blessed are the pure in heart, for they shall see God"* (Mt. 5:8).

They will feel Him near them on earth, and they will enjoy Him at close range in heaven.

Prayer — O Mary, guard my mind, my heart and my senses, in order that I may know, love and serve only Jesus and employ all my energies for His glory.

July 12

"Do you not know that you are God's temple and that God's Spirit dwells in you?... For God's temple is holy, and that temple you are" (1 Cor. 3:16-17).

"When we are in grace, we are a composite of body, soul, the Holy Spirit."   *Tertullian*

Reflection — *"How many will one day shout with surprise upon discovering who they had within them [the Blessed Trinity!] and they did not know it!"*
                                            Msgr. D'Hulst

Prayer — "O my Trinity, my All, my Happiness, I wish to spend my life speaking to You and listening to You!"   *Sr. Elizabeth of the Trinity*

July 13

"Whoever has found Jesus has found a great treasure, nay, the highest Good. Whoever loses Jesus loses more than if he had lost the entire universe."   *Imitation of Christ*

Reflection — *Many people live only on the surface of their soul; they never descend into its depths where God abides.*

Prayer — O most sacred Hearts of Jesus and Mary, grant me the grace to better know you, love you and imitate you. I offer you my whole heart that it may always be yours.

July 14

"If your right eye causes you to sin, pluck it out and throw it away; it is better that you lose one of your members than that your whole body be thrown into hell" (Mt. 5:29).

Reflection — *If you already had one foot inside heaven and stopped mortifying yourself, you could still damn your soul.*

Prayer — Lord, I detest my sins, which are an offense to Your Majesty, the cause of the death of Your divine Son and my spiritual ruin. I resolve to avoid all sin in the future.

July 15

Mary consecrated herself to God by a vow of virginity and spent her life at the temple in silence and prayer. She is co-redemptrix of the human race. The Church and the saints greet her thus: "You, O Mary, together with Jesus Christ, redeemed us."   *St. John Chrysostom*

Reflection — *"Paying homage to Mary means gathering great treasures for eternal life."*
                                Richard of St. Lawrence

Prayer — O Mother, accept me as your child. Accompany me throughout my life. Assist me daily and especially in the hour of my death.

July 16

Mary is the select spouse of the Holy Spirit. The angel explained to her: "The Holy Spirit will come upon you" (Lk. 1:35).

God chose for Mary the most pure of spouses, Joseph, who dedicated his entire life to the service of Jesus and Mary. An angel appeared to Joseph in a dream to reassure him of Mary's purity by revealing the sacred mystery accomplished in her.

Reflection — *As a reward for her virtue, Mary was assumed, body and soul, into heaven and crowned Queen of the universe.*

Prayer — O Mary, how great and how wonderful the day on which the august Trinity crowned you Queen of heaven and earth, dispenser of all graces and our most lovable Mother!

July 17

"The sole way to attain the heights of sound piety and interior life is the constant mortification of all the senses."   *St. John Baptist de La Salle*

"From the spirit of mortification rise pure thoughts, apostolic desires, generous will power."

Pope St. Leo the Great

Reflection — *"If you live according to the flesh you will die, but if by the Spirit you put to death the deeds of the body, you will live" (Rom. 8:13).*

Prayer — "O my God, come to me, fortify me, encourage me! You are my hope and my salvation, O Lord. I place my trust in You."   *Imitation of Christ*

July 18

Pure souls inspire good thoughts; their actions are almost like a sacrament.

Reflection — *"Never become discouraged when you are tempted, but pray with greater fervor; for God, with the temptation, has assured us of His grace."*   *Imitation of Christ*

Prayer — O Jesus, perfect example of mortification and purity, make me similar to You.

July 19

Purity is an enlightening virtue that introduces the intellect to knowledge, the soul to wisdom. It is a glorious virtue. "Purity makes man an angel and even superior to the angels."   *St. Ambrose*

Reflection — *"Die daily. Every day kill a little of the old man (the self), in order to make the new man (Christ) grow within us."*   Timothy Giaccardo

Prayer — Lord, give me Your light so that I may know myself as You will make me know myself on the day of Your judgment.

July 20

"While we live on earth we will never be without temptations because it is written that man's life on earth is a continual battle."

Imitation of Christ

Reflection — *"Everyone must watch and pray in order not to give occasion of victory to the devil who is always around, seeking to devour us."*

Imitation of Christ

Prayer — "Teach me, O Lord, your way
　　that I may walk in your truth;
　　direct my heart that it may fear your name.
I will give thanks to you, O Lord my God,
　　with all my heart,
　　and I will glorify your name forever
　　　(Ps. 86:11-12).*

July 21

"Impurity is a fire lighted by the devil. Lust is its fuel; pride, its flame; pleasure, its ashes; and hell, its end."   *St. Jerome*

"There is no remedy more efficacious in fighting impurity than meditation on Christ's passion."
St. Augustine

Reflection — *"Constant purity of the senses is a sublime martyrdom which will culminate in inestimable glory."*   *St. Francis of Assisi*

Prayer — O St. Michael the Archangel, together with your followers defend us in the battle. Be our protection against the malice and snares of the devil. May the Lord subdue him! And you, O prince of the heavenly host, thrust back into hell Satan and the other evil spirits who roam through the world seeking the ruin of souls.

July 22

"Corruption of the best is the most evil.... If he who has received an abundance of graces is ruined, he not only becomes corrupt; he becomes the worst."   *Pope St. Gregory the Great*

"All those who are damned go to hell because of impurity or at least with its traces."
St. Alphonsus

Reflection — *Let us remain attentive in the early stages of temptation, because it is easier to overcome the enemy while he is outside the door.*
Cf. Imitation of Christ

Prayer — O Divine Holy Spirit, to You I consecrate my heart. Guard and increase the divine life in me. Sustain me in the observance of the commandments and in the fulfillment of my duties.

July 23

Temptations are useful to man, even if they are strong and insistent. Through temptations, man humbles himself, purifies his soul, and becomes better instructed.   *Cf. Imitation of Christ*

Reflection — *"Making the Sign of the Cross frequently in times of temptation is a good means to chase the devil away."*   Don Orione

Prayer — O Lord, lead me not into temptation and deliver me from all evil.

July 24

"Mortification means a 'putting to death'—that is, the killing of something which must not be allowed to live."   James Alberione

Reflection — *"We must practice mortification with a view to meriting heaven and in imitation of Jesus Christ, whose entire life was a cross and martyrdom."*   James Alberione

Prayer — Heart of Jesus, I love you! Convert poor sinners.

July 25

"When it is a matter of overcoming obstacles to doing good, how much weakness is evident and how much inconstancy in effort! And how many times one lets his feelings and passions drag him down!"   *James Alberione*

Reflection — *How aptly St. Paul describes our weakness: "For I do not do the good I want, but the evil I do not want is what I do" (Rom. 7:19).*

Prayer — Lord Jesus, You know we have no faith in our own powers. In Your mercy grant that we may be defended against all adversity, through the intercession of St. Paul.

July 26

"It is easy to realize that corruption is the grave of faith. How could a vice-ridden soul, who despises virtue and finds his pleasure wallowing around in mud, ever bear to hear within himself a voice repeating that these things are prohibited by God, that one day He will judge each of us severely, and that eternal fire will be the punishment for unlawful pleasures?"   *James Alberione*

Reflection — *"How else can we explain the fact that young people who up until yesterday frequented the sacraments with delight have now stopped going to Mass, will not make their Easter duty and have joined the adversaries and mockers of religion? The fact is easily explained: they began to give up their faith when corruption made its first gains in their hearts!"*   *James Alberione*

Prayer — O Mary, turn your merciful eyes upon the more than four billion men living on this earth. God made you an apostle to give Jesus, Way and Truth and Life, to the world. By having recourse to you, they will find the road that leads to Jesus.

July 27

"Purity is beautiful precisely because it is the fruit of a struggle which often no one knows about, since it is waged within the heart, a struggle which does not last only for a moment but is continual."

James Alberione

Reflection — *"Among all the human battles we must wage on this earth, the most difficult are those for the virtue of purity. But because of these struggles, more merit is gained and more graces are given."*

James Alberione

Prayer — O Jesus, Way of sanctity, make me Your faithful imitator. Do not permit me to be separated from You. Grant that I may live eternally in the joy of Your love.

July 28

"Virginity of mind consists in not mixing good thoughts with thoughts which are not good. If one were to see a suggestive title or read the beginning of a bad book or article, he would not have committed a sin, but if he were to go ahead and continue to read, he would then be sinning."

James Alberione

Reflection — *"There is no need to be disturbed even if the battle is difficult and continuous. No matter what happens, there is no sin when it is not willed."*

James Alberione

Prayer — O Lord, enlighten the minds of many writers so that they may cease bringing ruin to souls through their teachings and perverse insinuations. May I seek to read and to distribute, as much as I am able, those writings whose salutary contents will help all to promote the greater glory of God, the exaltation of His Church, and the salvation of souls.

July 29

"Put to death what is earthly in you: immorality, impurity, passion, evil desire, and covetousness, which is idolatry. On account of these the wrath of God is coming" (Col. 3:5-6).

Reflection — *"This means preventing the faculties of soul and body from becoming instruments of evil.... This means continuing vigilance, prompt rejection of temptations, flight from occasions, control over pride, curiosity, sensuality, eating, laziness."*   James Alberione

Prayer — "Lord, keep my life, for I am devoted to you;
  save your servant who trusts in you.
Teach me, O Lord, your way
  that I may walk in your truth;
  direct my heart that it may fear your name" (Ps. 86:2, 11).*

July 30

"God united three all-pure souls—Jesus, Mary and Joseph—in the humble home of Nazareth. All hearts should turn to them as the examples and sources of all purity." *James Alberione*

Reflection — *"Let us remember that the Virgin of virgins brought the virtue of purity into the world, and to all who implore her aid she obtains the grace to preserve this divine virtue."* *James Alberione*

Prayer — O Lord, grant us the grace to know the Blessed Virgin Mary, Your most pure Mother; to imitate her, to love her, to pray to her always. Draw many souls to her maternal heart.

July 31

If you wish to find heaven on earth, associate with good persons, speak of edifying things. For by doing this you will be God's friend.

Reflection — *Those are happy who attend to their duties and to their salvation, by living in God and for God.*

Prayer — O God of love, grant that I may love You as I should, that is, with a love which surpasses all other loves.

AUGUST
Hope

August 1

Hope is the virtue by which we trust that our all-powerful and faithful God will bring us to heaven if we live as He asks us to live.

Reflection — *"Hope is the flame of our life, the smile of our sorrowful hours, the anchor in days of storm."*   Lacordaire

Prayer — My God, relying on Your infinite goodness and promises and on the merits of Jesus Christ, I hope to obtain life everlasting and the means to obtain it.

August 2

"The hope of the just brings them joy,
   but the expectation of the wicked
   comes to nought" (Prv. 10:28).*

Reflection — *"For the grace of God has appeared...training us to renounce irreligion and worldly passions, and to live sober, upright, and*

godly lives in this world, awaiting our blessed hope, the appearing of the glory of our great God and Savior Jesus Christ" (Ti. 2:11-13).

Prayer — "In Your mercy, O Lord, I have trusted; let me not be put to shame forever."   *Te Deum*

August 3

"The eyes of the Lord are upon those who fear
    him,
  upon those who hope for his kindness"
        (Ps. 33:18).*

Like a mantle of love, "kindness surrounds him who trusts in the Lord" (Ps. 32:10).*

Reflection — *Like exiles walking confidently toward their native land, "let us always sing the praises of God."*   St. Augustine

Prayer — "In you, O Lord, I take refuge;
  let me never be put to shame.
For you are my hope, O Lord;
  my trust, O God, from my youth" (Ps. 71:1, 5).*

August 4

"In order to save us from hell, Jesus Christ made reparation for our sins by suffering and dying on the cross, and He taught us how to live according to God's designs."   *Catechism of Pius X*

"Come to terms with him to be at peace.
...And upon your ways the light shall shine"
    (Job 22:21, 28).*

Reflection — *"This explains why we work and struggle as we do; our hopes are fixed on the living God who is the savior of all men, but especially of those who believe" (1 Tm. 4:10).* *

Prayer — Lord, I rejoice in my hope in You. Help me to be patient under trials and persevering in prayer (cf. Rom. 12:12).

August 5

"Jesus is a Mediator of blood, bound to the cross not with nails but with love."   *Robert Mauro*

"It is through him that you are believers in God, the God who raised him from the dead and gave him glory. Your faith and hope, then, are centered in God" (1 Pt. 1:21).*

Reflection — *"Christ cancelled with His blood the decree of our condemnation, nailing it to the cross" (cf. Col. 2:14).*   *St. Augustine*

Prayer — "A clean heart create for me, O God,
    and a steadfast spirit renew within me.
Cast me not out from your presence,
    and your holy spirit take not from me.
Give me back the joy of your salvation,
    and a willing spirit sustain in me" (Ps. 51:12-14).*

August 6

"Christian hope is the virtue by which we believe that our Lord has prepared for us an eternal reward in heaven, and that in His mercy, He will give us all the natural and supernatural helps, all the graces, in other words, needed to keep the commandments and to live up to the duties of our state in life so as to arrive at our eternal goal, our reward in heaven."   *James Alberione*

Reflection — *"We rely on the merits of Christ and on His promises. We do not doubt them because God is faithful. His promises are clear, and He will not fail to keep them."*   *James Alberione*

Prayer — O God, in You alone is my soul at rest; from You comes my hope. You alone are my rock and my salvation, my stronghold; I shall not be disturbed (cf. Ps. 62:5-6).

August 7

"In His infinite mercy, God has raised us to the supernatural level. Thus we are able to earn merit for heaven, as children of God: 'But if we are children, we are heirs as well: heirs of God, heirs with Christ' (Rom. 8:17).* How great is this call! How noble this vocation!"   *James Alberione*

Reflection — *"Our hope is founded in the first place on the omnipotence of God, because, according to his nature, man had no right to the supernatural happiness of heaven."*   *James Alberione*

Prayer — O God, Source of hope, fill me with all joy and peace in believing, so that through the power of the Holy Spirit I may have hope in abundance (cf. Rom. 15:13).

August 8

"Never be anxious for anything. Place yourself trustingly in God's hands; all that God permits and disposes is for our good. Always keep this in mind: trust in God."   *Servant of God, Mother Thecla Merlo*

Reflection — *"Let us seek to put all our effort in what we do. Yes, this is needed, really apply ourselves and on our part do all that we can; then trust in God, abandon ourselves in Him."*

Servant of God, Mother Thecla Merlo

Prayer — I will trust in You, O Lord. Yes, I will wait for You (cf. Is. 8:17).

August 9

"Take courage and be stouthearted,
    all you who hope in the Lord" (Ps. 31:25).*

"We trust in those who love us because we believe they are good, and yet many times we do not trust in God.... We need more confidence in God."   *Servant of God, Mother Thecla Merlo*

Reflection — *"Let us trust in God, have confidence in the Lord. He gives us all the graces that we need. They are already prepared."*

Servant of God, Mother Thecla Merlo

Prayer — O Jesus, You pleased the Father; You are my Model. Draw me to Yourself, and give me the grace to imitate You, especially in the virtue I need the most.

August 10

"I have the same hope in God...that there is to be a resurrection of the good and the wicked alike" (Acts 24:15).*

"And this hope will not leave us disappointed, because the love of God has been poured out in our hearts through the Holy Spirit who has been given to us" (Rom. 5:5).*

Reflection — *"Dearly beloved, we are God's children now;...we shall see him as he is. Everyone who has this hope based on him keeps himself pure, as he is pure" (1 Jn. 3:2-3).* *

Prayer — O Virgin Mary, radiant with joy, grant that we may believe in the happiness which God in His love wills to offer us.

August 11

"Each one of us should say: 'He came for me; Jesus came from heaven to save me, to give me graces and to merit heaven for me, to save my soul.' Never get discouraged, but trust in the Lord."

Servant of God, Mother Thecla Merlo

Reflection — *"Have much faith, unlimited faith in the goodness of God. The Lord is glorified more when we trust in Him than when we fear Him."*

Servant of God, Mother Thecla Merlo

Prayer — "By myself I can do nothing. But with God I can do all things. For the love of God I want to do all things. To Him honor and glory, to me the eternal reward."   *James Alberione*

August 12

"We boast of our hope for the glory of God. But not only that—we even boast of our afflictions! We know that affliction makes for endurance, and endurance for tested virtue, and tested virtue for hope. And this hope will not leave us disappointed" (Rom. 5:2-5).*

Reflection — *Let us not lose our confidence in God, which will bring us to a great reward (cf. Heb. 10:35).*

Prayer — "Why are you so downcast, O my soul? Why do you sigh within me?
Hope in God! For I shall again be thanking him, in the presence of my savior and my God" (Ps. 42:6).*

August 13

"Our hope is founded on the merits and promises of Jesus Christ. It can be said that in the Gospel, Jesus spoke more often of heaven than of anything else. How many times He returned to the subject of heaven and foretold the reward to be given to the just: 'Well done, good and faithful servant!' (Mt. 25:21)"
James Alberione

Reflection — *"Let us trust in God even when we feel we have done nothing to earn heaven. What counts is to have good will and confidence in the merits of Jesus."*
James Alberione

Prayer — Jesus, Divine Master, increase active hope in us and the desire to be found similar to You at the judgment, and to possess You forever in heaven.

August 14

Above all else, we hope to obtain heaven. Saint Augustine remarked: "Will not God give us any reward? Nothing but Himself. God's reward is the self-same God."

Reflection — *"Indeed, God is the supreme good and our eternal happiness. For this very reason saints renounced the goods of the earth and desired nothing but heaven."*   James Alberione

Prayer — Lord, I believe You created me for heaven, marked out for me the way to reach it, and await me there to give me the reward of the faithful servant. Grant me the strength to follow it generously.

August 15

Assumption—"Hope has faith as its foundation, and the more sound faith is, the higher hope rises. As a person grows in the knowledge of God, of God's goodness, power and fidelity, his heart expands and finds comfort in hoping." James Alberione

Reflection — *"In the Blessed Virgin there was no obstacle to this beautiful virtue: no sins, no attachments to creatures, to the world, or to herself. She rose freely and calmly to God, and in God she reposed."*   James Alberione

Prayer — O Mary, who abandoned your soul to happiness by offering it to God, grant that in our gift to God, our joy may be complete.

August 16

"During the passion, Mary's hope had to withstand many assaults. The angel had announced wondrous things about Jesus, but in the meantime He was the Victim of His persecutors; He was dragged from one tribunal to another, condemned to death and nailed to a cross. Nonetheless, Mary did not doubt. She was certain that He would reign in heaven and on earth, and she, 'hoping against hope, believed' (cf. Rom. 4:18)."   *James Alberione*

Reflection — *Let us learn to hope always, and together with Job let us say:*
"Slay me though he might, I will wait for him....
And this shall be my salvation..." (Job 13:15-16). *

Prayer — "To you I lift up my soul,
   O Lord, my God.
In you I trust; let me not be put to shame
   (Ps. 25:1-2).*

August 17

"Many times Jesus said to those who had recourse to Him for cures: 'Faith has made you whole: go in peace. Do you believe? If you can believe, everything is possible to you. Have faith, your sins have been forgiven."   *James Alberione*

Reflection — *"The measure of our hope is also the measure of graces. In order to be convinced of this it suffices to read the Gospel."*   *James Alberione*

Prayer — I pray to You, O Lord and Life: I adore You, I praise You, I beseech You, and I thank You for the gift of Sacred Scripture. With Mary, I shall remember and preserve Your words in my mind, and I shall meditate on them in my heart.

August 18

"God requests cooperation from His creatures; He does not want to do miraculously what can be obtained through prayer."   *James Alberione*

Reflection — *"Do everything that you can by yourself, as though you were not to expect anything from God, and trust in God for everything, as though you had done nothing."*   St. Ignatius of Loyola

Prayer — Live in our midst, O Mary. May sin never stain our soul. O Immaculate Virgin, crush the head of that insidious demon of discouragement.

August 19

"At Bethlehem, the Blessed Virgin hoped that the Lord would have prepared a refuge, but she searched for it throughout the city until she found shelter in the destined stable. The flight into Egypt, the loss of Jesus in the temple, and the crucifixion and death of Jesus were also occasions which revealed how operative Mary's hope was."

James Alberione

Reflection — *"Blessed are the souls who, after having done their utmost, abandon themselves in God and await help and reward from Him alone."*

James Alberione

Prayer — "The Lord is my light and my salvation:
  whom should I fear?
The Lord is my life's refuge;
  of whom should I be afraid?" (Ps. 27:1)*

August 20

"God is good! He wants to be called our Father.
He sacrificed His only Son for us. He wants us to inherit His paradise; He has placed innumerable
means of gaining eternal life at our disposal. He
has given us touching examples of His goodness in
the parables of the prodigal son, of the Good
Shepherd, of the lost sheep, as well as in the forgiving of Magdalene, the good thief, Matthew and
Peter."   *James Alberione*

Reflection — *God is faithful to His promises: "Ask,
and you will receive. Seek, and you will find. Knock,
and it will be opened to you" (Mt. 7:7).* "Let us hold
unswervingly to our profession which gives us hope,
for he who made the promise deserves our trust"
(Heb. 10:23).**

Prayer — "O Lord, your kindness reaches to
  heaven;
  your faithfulness, to the clouds.
Your justice is like the mountains of God;
...How precious is your kindness, O God!"
  (Ps. 36:6-8)*

August 21

Trust God especially in times of difficulty.
St. Paul writes: "We rejoice in our hope of sharing

the glory of God. More than that, we rejoice in our sufferings, knowing that suffering produces endurance, and endurance produces character, and character produces hope, and hope does not disappoint us" (Rom. 5:2-5).

Reflection — *"Lively is the courage of those who fear the Lord,*
 for they put their hope in their savior;
He who fears the Lord is never alarmed,
 never afraid; for the Lord is his hope"
   (Sir 34:13-14). *

Prayer — Lord, increase my faith and trust in You!

August 22

"After Jesus was buried in the sepulcher, Mary hastened His resurrection with her desires. Therefore, she retired in prayer; she did not join the pious women in searching among the dead for Him who was living, but she firmly hoped shortly to embrace her gloriously resurrected Son."

James Alberione

Reflection — *Let us pray to Mary: "After Jesus, you are my entire hope. Thus did St. Bernard call you, and thus do I want to call you."*   *James Alberione*

Prayer — Mother of holy hope and of life everlasting, pray for us!

August 23

"Mary stands out among the poor and humble of the Lord, who confidently hope for and receive salvation from Him. With her, the exalted Daughter of Zion, and after a long expectation of the promise, the times are fulfilled and the new Economy established, when the Son of God took a human nature from her, that He might in the mysteries of His flesh free man from sin."

Lumen gentium, no. 55

Reflection — *"And we desire each one of you to show the same earnestness in realizing the full assurance of hope until the end, so that you may not be sluggish, but imitators of those who through faith and patience inherit the promises" (Heb. 6:11-12).*

Prayer — O tender Mother Mary, Gate of heaven, Help of Christians, trust of the dying and hope even of the desperate, give me a repentant life, that I may have a holy death and one day join my voice to that of the saints to praise you in heaven.

August 24

"I am not working for a hope which can delude me (and certainly one who hopes in earthly goods will be deluded, since he will leave all when he dies). I work '... awaiting our blessed hope, the appearing of the glory of our great God and Savior Jesus Christ' (Ti. 2:13)."   *James Alberione*

Reflection — *"Let us think of heaven and rejoice. I am working for heaven!... Let us ask for and practice the virtue of hope more intensely, thinking of heaven in difficulties and temptations."*

James Alberione

Prayer — "How lovely is your dwelling place,
    O Lord of hosts!

My soul yearns and pines
    for the courts of the Lord.
My heart and my flesh
    cry out for the living God" (Ps. 84:2-3).*

August 25

"The Christian should always be inundated by a great joy and a living fervor. He who has his eyes on the goal quickens his step and does not get tired, or, if he does feel so (and this is human), he loves the very fatigue, and is courageous, fervent and enterprising for his own perfection and for his mission in life."

James Alberione

Reflection — *"Let us think of heaven. Let us think of it especially when we awaken in the morning: Today I will work for heaven."*   *James Alberione*

Prayer — O Mary, my Queen, my advocate, my sweetness, obtain for me holy perseverance.

August 26

"Hope is expressed in the prayer of petition. He who prays is saved; he who does not pray damns himself. Prayer is recommended more than five hundred times in Sacred Scripture."

James Alberione

Reflection — *"Trust in God! He is always our Father! Christ addressed Him by this name even when He was at the height of His sufferings: 'Father, into your hands I commit my spirit' (Lk. 23:46)."*

James Alberione

Prayer — "I will bless the Lord at all times;
   his praise shall be ever in my mouth.
Let my soul glory in the Lord;
   the lowly will hear me and be glad.
Glorify the Lord with me,
   let us together extol his name" (Ps. 34:2-4).*

August 27

"God is faithful to His Word given to the children of God. Furthermore, although full of sins and defects, we hope in the merits of our Savior. Through the death of Christ we are reconciled with God, and through Jesus we shall be saved."
                                        James Alberione

Reflection — *"In his letter to the Hebrews, St. Paul speaks of hope with a fervor that is moving. He wrote: 'Let us remain firm in our hope without wavering in any way. In virtue of the blood of our Lord Jesus Christ we acquire the right and the certainty of entering our celestial sanctuary.' Let us not lose hope, because it has great merits."*
                                        James Alberione

Prayer — O Jesus, our Master, I adore Your Heart, which has so greatly loved men and has not spared anything for them. I believe in Your infinite love for us.

August 28

"The words of our Lord Jesus Christ, 'Whatsoever you shall ask the Father in my name you shall receive it,' may be applied to him who hopes in God. The saints were accustomed to repeat: 'I have hoped in You, O Lord, I shall not be confounded in eternity.' "

James Alberione

Reflection — *"The fruits of hope are: a sweet serenity amid all sorrows; the constant considering of ourselves as pilgrims on this earth, who have a better fatherland awaiting us; the detachment from the goods of this world which are simply means; the constant effort to accumulate celestial treasures, and prayer to obtain the graces we need."*

James Alberione

Prayer — I take refuge in you, O Mary, as my supreme hope. Turn your eyes of mercy toward me. Bestow your most maternal care upon this your most needy child.

August 29

In the tabernacle is present the same Christ who is adored by the angels in heaven. Remain in God's presence in a spirit of deep humility. Make fervent acts of faith: "Lord, make me always believe more firmly in You." Make ardent acts of hope: "Lord, make me always trust in You more firmly." Make true acts of love: "Lord, make me love You more and more."

Reflection — *Jesus welcomes anyone who visits Him, and He receives the prayers of everyone regardless of personal worthiness.*

Prayer — "My God, detach my heart from earthly goods, and deeply root it in You, O sole, supreme Good!"

St. Augustine

August 30

"What will really make us happy is the possession of God. To possess God! Every good thing we hope for on this earth is uncertain. But the eternal good, God, is in no way doubtful. Whoever truly wants Him will possess Him."   *James Alberione*

Reflection — *"What joy this God will bring to the soul! Therefore, let us long for heaven. When faced with trying days, let us remember that what must impart courage is the reward: 'Each shall receive his wages according to his labor' (1 Cor. 3:8)."*
    James Alberione

Prayer — "Teach me, O Lord, your way
    that I may walk in your truth;
    direct my heart that it may fear your name.
I will give thanks to you, O Lord my God,
    with all my heart,
    and I will glorify your name forever"
    (Ps. 86:11-12).*

August 31

"Any soul who repents of his sin and turns to God will not be disillusioned; his desire will not be in vain. God will be his! And those who are constant in their love of God during life will have Him!"   *James Alberione*

Reflection — *Let us ask the Divine Master for the grace always to do the will of the Father as He did, and grow in the virtues of faith, hope and charity.*

Prayer — Lord, I trust in You; I put my trust in Your Word. With You, Lord, there is kindness and fullness of redemption (cf. Ps. 130:5-7).

SEPTEMBER
Faith

September 1

Rejoice "that the genuineness of your faith, more precious than gold which though perishable is tested by fire, may redound to praise and glory and honor at the revelation of Jesus Christ" (1 Pt. 1:7).

Reflection — *"Our faith is worthy of praise only when our deeds do not contradict the words we say."* Pope St. Gregory the Great

Prayer — "Lord, I believe in You, increase my faith." Pope Clement XI

September 2

"True faith is not merely the avoidance of sin; it is thinking, speaking and acting supernaturally." Timothy Giaccardo

"We will enjoy the eternal vision of God in heaven in proportion to the faith we possessed on earth." J. Scheeben

Reflection — *"We must always make frequent acts of faith, but, above all, in times of temptations and in danger of death."*   *Pope St. Pius X*

Prayer — Let us ask Jesus for an increase of faith: Lord, "I believe; help my unbelief!" (Mk. 9:24)

September 3

"Christ has been raised from the dead, the first fruits of those who have fallen asleep. We shall all be changed" (1 Cor. 15:20, 51).

"For we who have believed enter that rest" (Heb. 4:3).

Reflection — *"If for this life only we have hoped in Christ, we are of all men most to be pitied" (1 Cor. 15:19).*

Prayer — "I believe, O Lord. Grant that I may continually grow in faith."   *James Alberione*

September 4

St. Paul had fought and persecuted Jesus Christ, but Jesus stopped him and Paul felt a strong hand upon him against which he could not rebel. He asked that invisible Power: "Who are you?" The invisible Power answered: "I am Jesus Christ." And St. Paul believed. He recognized Jesus as his Lord, and submitted himself to His desires.

Reflection — *Nearing his death, St. Paul wrote: "I have kept the faith." He was persecuted for his faith, but he never doubted for an instant and preached it incessantly.*

Prayer — Lord, make my faith grow to the point of living by it and sharing it with my neighbor.

September 5

Faith renders us acceptable to God; refusal to believe takes us away from Him.

"No condition is more pitiful than that of the unbeliever; in his soul there is always night."

St. Augustine

Reflection — *Let us find comfort in the words of our Lord: "He who believes in the Son has eternal life..." (Jn. 3:36).*

Prayer — Sacred Heart of Jesus, I believe in Your love for me!

September 6

"Faith is increased with exercise; the person who allows his faith to remain inactive deserves to lose it."   *St. Vincent de Paul*

"Faith is uprooted from our souls predominantly by pride and by impurity."   *Lacordaire*

Reflection — *Faith is a torch that God hands to us lighted; if we let the flame die out, we cannot light it again by ourselves.*

Prayer — O Heart of Jesus, I place my trust in You.

September 7

"The loss of faith is the worst punishment of God, and He permits it to befall those who greatly abuse His graces."   *Cardinal Gomes of Thomas*

"If a person with faith already has one foot in heaven, then it is possible to say that a person who has lost faith through his own fault already has both feet in hell."   *Lacordaire*

Reflection — *Pray frequently for the infidels and unbelievers: "They are truly the most unfortunate."*
                                        St. Teresa of Avila

Prayer — "Lord, You know that we are nothing, that wherever we look we see only our own limitations, our lack of strength, of faith, of charity, of hope, and our helplessness. Give us the grace to know how to walk under the guidance of St. Paul."
                                        James Alberione

September 8

Faith is necessary in order to be saved: "...Without faith it is impossible to please [God]" (Heb. 11:6).

"He who believes and is baptized will be saved; but he who does not believe will be condemned" (Mk. 16:16).

Reflection — *Faith is a gratuitous gift of God, which we cannot merit of ourselves"*   *St. Irenaeus*

Prayer — O Lord, increase our faith.

September 9

"The test of faith means believing in God's love. The test of love means loving God. The test of fidelity means being faithful to His Word and observing His commandments. Having passed the test, heaven is ours."   *James Alberione*

Reflection — *"Whoever is without faith is more unhappy than those without sight; the latter cannot see the world, but the former cannot see the Creator of the world."*   Cardinal Maffi

Prayer — O Jesus Divine Master, grant that I may one day find myself in heaven with a multitude of saved souls as my joy and my crown.

September 10

"It is faith that gives to the soul the eye with which it will be able to contemplate God in heaven for all eternity."   *St. Francis de Sales*

There is but "one Lord, one faith, one baptism, one God and Father of us all, who is above all" (Eph. 4:5-6).

Reflection — *"The billions of infidels in the world ought to weigh on our hearts like a mountain."*

Cardinal Maffi

Prayer — O Shepherd of our souls, turn Your merciful eyes upon the billions of men living on this earth.

September 11

"The Scripture says, 'No one who believes in him will be put to shame.' And how are they to believe in him of whom they have never heard? And how are they to hear without a preacher?" (Rom. 10:11, 14)

Reflection — *"Pray therefore the Lord of the harvest to send out laborers into his harvest" (Mt. 9:38).*

Prayer — O divine Heart of Jesus, multiply religious vocations.

September 12

"Faith is infused in the soul in Baptism, and is increased by all the other sacraments. Nevertheless growth in faith includes the exercise of this virtue."
James Alberione

Reflection — *"We must instruct ourselves more and more in the eternal truths. This we do by reading the Bible, by deepening the study of our religion, by spiritual reading."*   *James Alberione*

Prayer — Good Jesus, impress upon my heart lively sentiments of faith.

September 13

"God wills or permits everything for only one end, that we may reach heaven. 'We know that in everything God works for good with those who love him' (Rom. 8:28)."
James Alberione

Reflection — *"May we always look at things in God, with serenity, lovingly accepting His will."*

James Alberione

Prayer — O Lord, convert me once and for always. Give me a repentant life, that I may have a holy death and one day join my voice to that of the saints to praise You in heaven.

September 14

"To love Mary ardently is a sign of lively faith and a certain pledge of salvation."

Pelbarto di Temesvar

"Who fears to honor Mary too much when God has exalted her above the choirs of angels in the kingdom of the Blessed?"   *St. Louis de Montfort*

"Whoever does not love the Blessed Mother a great deal loves her Son little!"   *St. Bernard*

Reflection — *"Let us venerate Mary with all the ardor of our heart, because God takes such great pleasure in it."*   *St. Louis de Montfort*

Prayer — "O Lord, help me to have the three necessary conditions for prayer: faith, humility and perseverance."   *James Alberione*

September 15

He came "to give knowledge of salvation to his people in the forgiveness of their sins" (Lk. 1:77).

Only He is called the Word of God; only He has words of eternal life (cf. Rv. 19:13; Jn. 6:69).

"Neither be called masters, for you have one master, the Christ" (Mt. 23:10).

Reflection — *"It is important that we meditate upon the truths of faith. It is then that these truths go from our mind to our will and heart.*

James Alberione

Prayer — O Christ, You are the sole Sun of truth that enlightens minds, and shines through the darkness of night, showing us the way to salvation.

September 16

"A life of faith leads us to desire an increase of grace, and thus, to make use of every means that may bring it about. And with this goes the desire to perfect our union with God in Jesus Christ."

James Alberione

Reflection — *"To stir up our faith at all times, we must examine ourselves on this virtue."*

James Alberione

Prayer — O Jesus, Way of sanctity, make me Your faithful imitator.

September 17

"Heaven is promised to those who love God not in words but in deeds, i.e., in observance of His commandments."   *James Alberione*

Reflection — *"Now is the time to ask the Lord for a living faith in heaven, for the grace to know Him well in this life and for the grace to make Him known to others."*   *James Alberione*

Prayer — Lord, be my eternal Reward!

September 18

"In the beginning was the Word, and the Word was with God, and the Word was God" (Jn. 1:1).

"All things were made through him, and without him was not anything made that was made" (Jn. 1:3).

"And the Word became flesh and dwelt among us.... We have beheld his glory, glory as of the only Son from the Father" (Jn. 1:14).

"No one has ever seen God; the only Son, who is in the bosom of the Father, he has made him known" (Jn. 1:18).

Reflection — *"The Son of God became man to save sinful man. This was His constant concern: to save, bringing truth, holiness, and worship of the true God."*   *James Alberione*

Prayer — O Jesus, obtain for us a lively, firm and active faith—faith which saves and produces saints, faith in the Church, in the Gospel, in eternal life.

September 19

Jesus Christ is the second Person of the Blessed Trinity, that is, the Son of God made Man.

He suffered under Pontius Pilate, was crucified, died, and was buried, but on the third day He rose again from the dead.

After forty days, He ascended into heaven, where He sits at the right hand of God, the Father almighty.

From thence He shall come to judge the living and the dead. At the end of the world, He will give to each one the eternal reward or punishment for the good or evil each has performed in life.

Reflection — *"Blessed...are those who hear the word of God and keep it!"* (Lk. 11:28)

"Heaven and earth will pass away, but my words will not pass away" (Mt. 24:35).

Prayer — O Lord, help me to be a doer of Your Word, and not a hearer only, deceiving myself.

September 20

"...God spoke of old to our fathers by the prophets; but in these last days he has spoken to us by a Son..." (Heb. 1:1-2).

Jesus "reflects the glory of God and bears the very stamp of his nature..." (Heb. 1:3).

Reflection — *Jesus is the only-begotten Son of God come on the earth to give life, the most abundant life, to us: the life of grace.*

Prayer — O Lord, I thank You, because by dying on the cross You merited life for us, which You give us in Baptism and nourish in Holy Communion and in the other sacraments. Live in us, O Jesus, with the outpouring of the Holy Spirit, so that we may love You more and more!

September 21

To achieve perfect love of God, there must be a proportionate depth of faith.

Reflection — *"Without the foundation of faith, love cannot last; it is merely sentimentalism."*

James Alberione

Prayer — Infuse in me, O divine Spirit, a deep, constant, joyful faith. May it be the sun of my life, the lantern for the path to eternity, a gift of Your tender love.

September 22

It is a truth of faith that, whether our lives are long or short, we can save ourselves.

Reflection — *"See how far your faith must go—to believing that notwithstanding our sins we can become holy."*

James Alberione

Prayer — O omnipotent, adorable, venerable, tremendous, one and greatest God, I bless You and I glorify You in eternity!

September 23

Let us recall the duties of our Baptism: to believe, to observe the divine law, to serve God.

Reflection — *"Thinking of this we can make an examination of conscience that embraces the whole complex of duties which Christians have."*

James Alberione

Prayer — We praise You, we bless You, we adore You, we glorify You, we give You thanks for Your immense glory!

September 24

"Faith is belief in heaven, even though we have not yet seen it; belief in Christ's real presence in the Blessed Sacrament, even though we do not see Him."   James Alberione

Reflection — *"Every fragment of the white host contains Jesus, that is, it contains God, the Infinite, the All! With what reverence should we approach the Eucharist!"*   St. Julian Eymard

Prayer — Kneeling before Jesus present in the Tabernacle, repeat with great faith the words of St. Thomas: "My Lord and my God!" (Jn. 20:28)

September 25

"We believe in only one God, one in Trinity and three in Unity, without mingling their Persons nor separating their nature.

"In fact, one is the person of the Father, one is the person of the Son, one, the person of the Holy Spirit; however, their glory and their majesty are equal.

"The Father is uncreated, the Son is uncreated, the Holy Spirit is uncreated; still, they are not three Uncreated Beings, but only one Uncreated God.

"The Father is immense, the Son is immense, the Holy Spirit is immense, yet there are not three Immense Beings, but only one.

"The Father is omnipotent, the Son is omnipotent, the Holy Spirit is omnipotent, yet there are not three All-powerful Beings, but only one Omnipotent God.

"The Father is God, the Son is God, the Holy Spirit is God, and still there are not three Gods, but only one God."   *Athanasian Creed*

Reflection — *Let us adore the infinite wisdom of Jesus, uncreated Truth, Master of all peoples.*

Let us thank Him for the flaming truths He revealed to us during His public life.

Let us thank Him for having sent the Apostles to teach all nations, and for continuing their mission by means of the priests (cf. Mt. 28:19).

Prayer — Holy, holy, holy are You, Lord of hosts (cf. Is. 6:3).

September 26

"Faith makes our minds holy. Through faith the Christian can elevate himself above reason."

James Alberione

Reflection — *"Faith makes us believe in God's Providence in all things."*   *James Alberione*

Prayer — May the one and holy Trinity, Creator and Governor of all things, be blest now and always forever and ever!

September 27

"What is impossible to men is possible to God."

James Alberione

Reflection — *"Do, therefore, what is 'impossible' for you, and by God's grace it will become possible due to His mercy and power."*   *James Alberione*

Prayer — We believe, submitting our whole mind to You and to the Church; and we condemn all that the Church condemns.

September 28

He who comes "to God must believe that he exists and that he rewards those who seek him" (Heb. 11:6).

Reflection — *"He truly believes who puts what he believes into practice."*   *Pope St. Gregory the Great*

Prayer — Lord Jesus, grant that whoever draws near You, in search of Your benefits, may rejoice in receiving them.

September 29

"Let us deepen our faith in the resurrection of Jesus Christ, and witness to it before the world."

James Alberione

Reflection — *"If you confess with your lips that Jesus is Lord and believe in your heart that God raised him from the dead, you will be saved"* *(Rom. 10:9).*

Prayer — I firmly believe, my God, in the resurrection of Jesus Christ.

September 30

"Faith is the foundation and root of justification. Just as a root not only sustains a tree, but also provides nourishment to produce leaves, flowers and fruit, so too faith not only maintains spiritual life, but also nourishes it by inspiring us to make acts of hope and charity." *James Alberione*

Reflection — *"Upon faith depend Christian perfection, the religious vocation, and apostolic zeal."*

James Alberione

Prayer — Virgin most faithful, pray for us.

Litany of Loretto

OCTOBER
Devotion to Mary

October 1

"Everything of beauty, purity, and holiness that a creature could possibly possess, God gave to His Mother."
St. Ephrem

"As Mother of the Word Incarnate, Mary was elevated to a certain equality with the heavenly Father."
St. Bernard

"In fact, she was the earthly Mother of Him whose Father in heaven is God." *St. Thomas, Bishop*

"Therefore, she had a natural power over the Lord for everything." From Him she obtains everything she desires.
Gerson

Reflection — *"The more Mary is praised, the more God is honored, the more souls are purified and the more the kingdom of Jesus Christ is extended."*
James Alberione

Prayer — Let everyone who believes in your divine maternity, O Mary, feel your protection.

October 2

"Mary is so holy that she is the most perfect model of all the virtues to all mankind." *St. Ambrose*

"Mary is the mighty rod of Aaron which conquers the powers of hell."   *St. Peter Damian*

Reflection — *"Praising Mary is every person's duty."*   *James Alberione*

Prayer — "O Mary, you are a garden well guarded from danger. Never did the hand of sin enter it to steal its flowers."   *St. Bernard*

October 3

Let us consider the very beautiful and well-deserved praise that Elizabeth addressed to Mary: "Blessed is she who believed that there would be a fulfillment of what was spoken to her from the Lord" (Lk. 1:45).

Because she believed in the coming of the Messiah, she hastened it with her ardent invocations.

Because she believed the words of the angel, she was chosen to be the Mother of the Word made flesh.

She believed in the power of the Holy Spirit and was selected to be His spouse.

Because she believed in the divinity of Jesus, she became the confidante of His heart.

Because she believed in Christ's mission of salvation, she became the co-redemptrix of the whole human race.

Because she had faith in the mystery of Calvary, she rejoiced in the triumph of the resurrection.

Reflection — *"In every necessity, let us confidently have recourse to this Mother of mercy; she will always grant our request."*   James Alberione

Prayer — "O Blessed Virgin, Mother of God, from the depths of my heart I praise and extol you as the purest, the fairest, the holiest creature of all God's handiwork."   James Alberione

October 4

"Mary is holier than the saints, loftier than the heavens, more glorious than the cherubim, more venerable than any other creature."   St. Germanus

"She is like an incomparable miracle, the climax of all miracles, and an unfathomable abyss of graces."   Pope Pius IX

"Remove the sun that illumines the world and from where will light be obtained? Remove Mary and what will remain but darkness and the shadow of death?"   St. Bernard

Reflection — *"All the prophets desired Mary; let us, too, desire her and pray to her."*   James Alberione

Prayer — Hail, O great Queen! Never permit me to forget you, and you will never forget me!

October 5

Hail, O Mother of Christ, companion during His passion and Queen of glory!

"Hail, O precious daisy, that became an inextinguishable light in God's heaven."

St. Cyril of Alexandria

"With only a slight gesture, you, who are all-powerful before God, destroyed the list of my many sins."   *Eutimius Zigabeno*

Reflection — *"Whoever is a true servant of Mary is as sure of heaven as if he were already there."*

Guerrico Abate

Prayer — O fortunate Mother and most pure Virgin, intercede for us that we may reach the door of salvation.

October 6

"Who is this coming up from the desert
leaning on her beloved?" (Sg. 8:5)**

"Come from Lebanon, my promised bride,
come from Lebanon, come on your way"
    (Sg. 4:8).**

"Hail, O heavenly sovereign, you who obtain
the scepter for your servants!"   *St. Ephrem*

"You are the staircase by which God descended
to us and with which we must ascend again to
Him."   *St. Bonaventure*

You are "the little spring that became a river,
the light that shone, the sun, the flood of water"
(Est. 10:6).**

Confronted by so much greatness, my tongue
will no longer know how to speak: "My praise will
be silence!"   *St. Thomas of Villanova*

Reflection — *"Let us try to possess in some manner the sublime virtues of the great Mother of God, and be, insofar as it is possible, living images of Mary."*
James Alberione

Prayer — O Mother of God, so great and so holy, remember me, a poor sinner!

October 7

Our Lady of the Rosary—"Mary's name, like the name of Jesus, is joy to the heart, a drop of honey to the mouth, a delightful melody to the ear."
St. Anthony of Padua

"The thought of Mary brings joy to the afflicted, fervor to the weak, and calls the way-ward back to the path of salvation."
Ludolph of Saxony

"Heaven and earth know no other name so full of grace, of hope, and sweetness, after that of your Son!"
Abbot Francone

"The devils fear your power, O Mary, and at the sound of your name they flee as from a devouring fire."
Thomas á Kempis

"The good angels rejoice upon hearing your name, and they run to help the soul who called upon you, O sweet Mother!" *Dionysius the Carthusian*

Reflection — *"Let us resolve to pray to the Blessed Virgin, especially with the recitation of the rosary. Mary will reign in our heart and when Mary is with us, what can we fear?"*
James Alberione

Prayer — Queen of the holy rosary, pray for us.
Litany of Loretto

October 8

Imagine the torment in Mary's heart when Jesus was lost in the temple and during the last months of Jesus' life when His passion was drawing near.

"During His passion, Mary suffered in her heart all the pains that Jesus suffered in His body. For this reason, God exalted her so greatly."

St. Bernard

"As the roses grow, so grow the thorns. In the same way, as Mary grew older, her sufferings became more and more acute."   *St. Brigid*

Reflection — *"Let us resolve to avoid every sin and, as much as possible, to make reparation for the offenses given to the hearts of Jesus and Mary."*

James Alberione

Prayer — O most powerful Queen, make me always remember you so that you will never forget me!

October 9

"Who is she that rises like a plant of vines leaning against a great tree, supported by the divine Word?"   *St. Ambrose*

"Mother of God! If we could only understand the ocean of greatness contained within these words, we would remain in ecstasy before Mary for all our life!"   *Cardinal Peter De Berulle*

"The privilege of becoming Mother of God conferred upon the most Holy Virgin a certain infinity."   *St. Thomas of Villanova*

Reflection — *"Mary is our wise counselor. Let us have recourse to her in every doubt, fear and temptation."*
                                          James Alberione

Prayer — "O Mary, dearly beloved Mother, how close to God you are and how utterly filled with Him! Obtain for me the grace of loving my Jesus; obtain for me the grace of loving you."
                                          James Alberione

October 10

"After the hypostatic union of Christ with God it is impossible to find any other more intimate union with Him than that of His Mother."
                    Dionysius the Carthusian

"In fact, she could never become more intimately united with God, without becoming another God herself!"   *St. Albert the Great*

"Although she was so great, Mary was at the same time so humble that she merited to become the ladder by which God descended upon earth."
                                          St. Augustine

"With her 'Fiat,' the Virgin merited primacy over all things, dominion over the universe, the scepter of an eternal kingdom."   *St. Bernard*

Reflection — *"Mary brought blessings. Following her example, let us try to do good to everyone, wherever we go."*   *James Alberione*

Prayer — "Hail, O radiant dawn and resplendent dove, untouched by the poisonous tongue of the serpent!"   *Origen*

October 11

"God created two great prodigies in the world: the Blessed Virgin and the priest."   *Venerable Olier*

"Mary is the mysterious field mentioned in the parables, in which a very precious treasure was discovered: Jesus, the Treasure of the Father."

St. Bonaventure

Reflection — *Let us turn with confidence to the Mother of God, that we may receive help in time of need.*

Prayer — "O sweetest Thief of hearts, come and steal my heart, too!"   *St. Bernard*

October 12

"The queen takes her place at your right hand in gold of Ophir" (Ps. 45:10).*

She is pure as the snow, "as beautiful as the moon, as resplendent as the sun..." (Sg. 6:10).*

She was "clothed with the sun, with the moon under her feet, and on her head a crown of twelve stars" (Rv. 12:1).

God chose her and preferred her above all others and placed on her head a crown of glory.

"Mary saw above her only God and Christ; and below her she saw all other creatures."

St. Peter Canisius

"Her throne is so radiant with light that in paradise she is an additional paradise."   *St. Peter Canisius*

Reflection — *"Let us ask the Blessed Virgin to fashion our hearts according to hers."*

James Alberione

Prayer — "O dearest and most clement Virgin Mother, you are our hope, most sure and sacred in God's sight, to whom be honor and glory."

James Alberione

October 13

"Jesus, Son of Mary, has no likeness among men, nor has Mary any likeness among women. He is the most beautiful of the living; she is a splendid dawn rising."   *St. Bruno*

"By saying that Mary is the Mother of God, we declare of her a greatness that surpasses all the other grandeurs that we can imagine after God."

Edmero

"God could have made a greater world and a higher heaven, but He could never make a mother greater than His own Mother."   *Conrad of Saxony*

Reflection — *Let us honor, invoke and defend Mary's name.*

Prayer — "Immaculate Virgin, who directed every movement of your most pure heart toward God, obtain for me the grace to hate sin with all my heart and to live in perfect resignation to the will of God."   *James Alberione*

October 14

"The heart of Mary! What a marvelous door God has opened for us to enter heaven!"

Cardinal Peter De Berulle

"Her heart is the temple of divine mercy where every sin finds pardon."   *Father William Chaminade*

"Whoever lives in Mary's heart becomes flooded with the Holy Spirit, because her heart is overflowing with Him."   *Timothy Giaccardo*

"Mary's heart is the cause of our joy; it has a joy for our every sorrow."   *Gabriel Perboyre*

Reflection — *"Let us unceasingly concentrate upon our celestial Mother's perfect life, so as to reproduce it in our actions."*   *James Alberione*

Prayer — "O most tender Virgin, make us feel the sweetness of your motherly heart and the might of your intercession with Jesus."   *James Alberione*

October 15

"Mary's heart is like the infinite love of God that has become tangible."   *St. John Eudes*

"It was with the blood of Mary's heart that the most sweet Heart of Jesus was formed."

Timothy Giaccardo

"Enormous was the flood of divine grace in Mary, but no less extravagant was the love with which she offered herself to the Giver of grace."

St. John Eudes

"The many caresses Jesus gave her made Mary always more holy and more divine."

St. Peter Canisius

Reflection — *"As Mary, let us make Jesus loved by many souls."*   *James Alberione*

Prayer — Draw us near you, O Immaculate One, and we will follow you in the perfume of your virtues.

October 16

"Mary became conqueror of errors and heresies, the powerful shield of the Catholic Church."   *St. Ephrem*

"Keep her name on your lips, her love in your heart. Imitate her, and her powerful intercession will surround you. Following her, you will not stray. Praying to her, you will ward off disaster and despair. Meditate on her and you will not err. Cling to her and you cannot fall."   *St. Bernard*

Reflection — *"If our necessities are great, Mary's power is also great; and if we ask with faith, we shall certainly receive."*   James Alberione

Prayer — "Mary most holy, Mother of goodness and mercy, obtain for me the grace to call upon you more frequently!"   James Alberione

October 17

"By becoming Mother of God, Mary belongs to the order of hypostatic union; hence, she participates in the infinite sanctity of God."

Dionysius the Carthusian

"By appointing her to this highest dignity, God sanctified her beforehand in such a way as to render her fit for it."   *St. Thomas*

Reflection — Whoever goes to Mary will find Jesus.

Prayer — "O Virgin blest, you were born for the salvation of the entire world!"   *St. John Damascene*

October 18

"God gathered together all the waters of earth and called them seas. He gathered together all the graces of heaven and called them Mary."

St. Louis de Montfort

"You dressed the divine Sun like a cloud, and He vested you with His light."   *St. Bernard*

"Wisdom has built her house in you; she has set up her seven columns: the seven gifts of the Holy Spirit."   *St. Bernard*

"You were the divine mouth which the Father used to pronounce audibly the Word, His divine Son."   *Fr. D'Argentan*

"You are a garden rich with heavenly blossoms of the most glorious beauty!"   *St. Bernard*

Reflection — *"The spirit of Mary is needed in our lives: the supernatural spirit of humility, love, and confidence."*   *James Alberione*

Prayer — Hail Mary, lily among thorns, purest dove, guiding star for the shipwrecked, eternal joy in the heavens!

October 19

"Mary became the Mother of God through a motive of mercy, that is, to give her help to us miserable creatures."   *Richard of St. Victor*

"Who is able to measure the length or width, the height or depth of her mercy? It fills the heavens and the earth!"   *St. Bernard*

"Your adversary the devil prowls around like a roaring lion, seeking someone to devour" (1 Pt. 5:8).

Who will be able to escape safely through so many snares? "Only he who, on the tempestuous sea of life, is carried aboard the divine vessel, who is Mary."   *Richard of St. Lawrence*

Reflection — *"Nothing assures us of perseverance except praying to Mary assiduously. But can we pray all the time? I say that we can, if we love Mary very much."*   St. Alphonsus Liguori

Prayer — "In you, O Lady, I hope; may I not be confounded in eternity!"   *St. Louis de Montfort*

October 20

"Mary's soul was so full of beauty that God, the Eternal Splendor, fell in love with it and chose her to be His Mother."   *St. Ambrose*

God loved her so much that, for her love, He sent an angel on earth "with the decree of peace awaited for so many years."   *Dante*

"Mary was a sea of all the heavenly delights, a miracle of all miracles."   *John Giemetra*

"Mary practices the most sublime virtues in the most sublime manner, unattainable by any other creature."   *St. Ambrose*

Reflection — *"Repeat this little prayer often: 'Jesus, Mary!' It is easy to remember, sweet to think of, powerful to protect us!"*   Imitation of Christ

Prayer — Hail, O most holy name, O radiant lamp given to men absorbed in the darkness of evil, to lighten their way, comfort and warm them!

October 21

"Jesus Christ was born of the Virgin Mary, who was called—and really is—the Mother of God."
Catechism of Pius X

"After God, it is impossible to think of anything greater than His Mother."   *St. Anselm*

"By selecting Mary to be His Mother, God loved her more than all the angels and saints together."
Bossuet

Reflection — *"Let us honor the sublime Virgin, she who is the holy Mother of God, and let us reap from her a salutary lesson: the lesson of love."*
James Alberione

Prayer — "Most glorious Virgin, chosen by God to be the Mother of the eternal Word made flesh, be my guide and counselor in this vale of tears."
James Alberione

October 22

"The divine maternity flooded Mary with a quantity of grace superior to all the grace in heaven."   *St. Bonaventure*

"The love of all the mothers for their children is only a shadow in comparison to the love Mary bears for each one of us."   *Father Niesemberg*

Reflection — *Imagine the sweet meeting between Jesus and His Mother when, at the end of her earthly pilgrimage, she was assumed body and soul into heaven!*

Prayer — Pray, O Mary, pray and never cease to pray, until you shall see me safe in paradise, where

I shall be sure of possessing and loving my God together with you, my dearest Mother, forever and ever."

James Alberione

October 23

"If all the stars were tongues and all the grains of sand were words, they still would not be able to say all the glories bestowed on Mary's soul by God."

St. Thomas Villanova

"Mary is the paradise where Jesus became flesh through the workings of the Holy Spirit."

St. Louis de Montfort

"At her birth, Mary was a dawn; in life she was a light; at death she was a sun."

Abbot Robert

"She was born from love, she lived for love.... She is the Mother of beautiful love."

St. Bernardine of Siena

Reflection — *"We owe Mary a deep love, for she gave us Jesus who is all our strength and all our love."*

James Alberione

Prayer — "O Mary, make me live in God, with God and for God."

James Alberione

October 24

"With Mary's protection, there is nothing to fear. Under her leadership, you will succeed. With her encouragement, all is possible.

St. Bernard

"Devotion to the Virgin, far from subtracting from the glory of God, leads us rather directly back to that Author of all good who has willed her to be so great and so pure."

Pope Pius XII

Reflection — *"Let us beg Mary for her spirit of piety."*
James Alberione

Prayer — "Receive me, O Mary, Mother, Teacher and Queen among those whom you love, nourish, sanctify, and guide in the school of Jesus Christ, the Divine Master. He entrusted Himself wholly to you from the Incarnation to the Ascension. For me this is doctrine, example and an ineffable gift. I too place myself entirely into your hands."
James Alberione

October 25

"By the will of God, the most Blessed Virgin Mary was inseparably joined with Christ in accomplishing the work of man's redemption, so that our salvation flows from the love of Jesus Christ and His sufferings intimately united with the love and sorrows of His Mother. It is, then, highly fitting that, after due homage has been paid to the most Sacred Heart of Jesus, Christian people, who have obtained divine life from Christ through Mary, manifest similar piety and the love of their grateful souls for the most loving heart of our heavenly Mother."
Pope John XXIII

Reflection — *"Let us learn from Mary to live in humility: Only he who knows how to humble himself will be exalted by God."*
James Alberione

Prayer — Hail, O Queen of Paradise,
"You are the glory of Jerusalem!
You are the great pride of Israel!
You are the highest honour of our race!"
  (Jdt. 15:10)**

October 26

"The soul of Mary not only was all beautiful but, after the Incarnation of the Word, it was the greatest work created by God."   *St. Peter Damian*

"Divine grace did not descend into her soul drop by drop, as it did in the saints, but in the form of abundant rain over fleece."   *St. Alphonsus Liguori*

"She possessed in absolute fullness what the saints possessed only in minimum measure."
St. Bonaventure

Rejoice with me because, as lowly as I was, I was pleasing to the most high God and from my womb was born the God-man.

Reflection — *"Pious souls devoted to Mary are more courageous in sacrifice, more prompt to obey, more modest in their behavior, and more ardent in charity; in short, they make greater spiritual progress."*   James Alberione

Prayer — "Hail, O most brilliant star, font of eternal light; open the doors of glory for us. Amen."
St. Jerome

October 27

The Lord elected her and favored her and made her dwell in His tabernacle.

"Mary is the dawn of God because, just as the dawn marks the end of darkness and the beginning of day, so Mary indicates the end of vices and the beginning of virtue."   *Pope St. Innocent III*

"Mary is pleasing to God but as terrifying to the devil as an unvanquished army prepared for war."
Abbot Rupert

God loved Mary so much that He gave her the keys to His heart. "No one can go to God without Mary drawing him."   *Richard of St. Victor*

"The Holy Spirit inflamed her like the fire making iron red-hot, and in her remained nothing but that divine flame."   *St. Ildephonsus*

Reflection — *"Let us take refuge in Mary; she is a powerful, merciful, and understanding Mother."*
                    James Alberione

Prayer — "Hail, O radiant column, that guides men in the desert of life to their goal: Christ!"
                    Didimus of Alexandria

October 28

"As the sun so strongly surpasses the splendor of the stars that the stars disappear before it, so Mary surpasses in sanctity all the celestial court."
                    St. Peter Damian

"If she were not so holy as she is, how could God appoint her to be the ladder of paradise, the advocate of the world, mediatrix between Him and us?"   *St. Lawrence Justinian*

Reflection — *"Let us belong to Mary! In every age and condition of spirit let us hope in her. May the penitent, the proficient, and the perfect confide in Mary. Mary is the Mother of all."*   *James Alberione*

Prayer — "Hail, graceful and charming paradise of God, more fragrant than the most beautiful lilies!"   *St. Germanus*

October 29

In Mary, divine Goodness proposes for our imitation an admirable example truly adaptable to our own lives.

"She, having our very same nature, does not dazzle us, as Jesus does with the splendors of His divinity."   *Pope Leo XIII*

"The saints were exemplars of some particular virtue; Mary is the exemplar of all the virtues in the highest degree."   *St. Thomas Aquinas*

Reflection — *"Let us imitate Mary most holy. We shall thus find the practice of virtue much easier."*
                                        James Alberione

Prayer — Blessed be the name of Mary, Virgin and Mother!   *The Divine Praises*

October 30

"When Jesus saw his mother, and the disciple whom he loved standing near, he said to his mother, 'Woman, behold, your son!' Then he said to the disciple, 'Behold, your mother!'" (Jn. 19:26-27)

"Mary, Mother of the Head of the Mystical Body, is also Mother of all its members."

                                        Pope St. Pius X

"Jesus, Son of grace, was born to her amid the hymns of angels; we, children of sin, were born to her amid His enemies' shouts: Crucify Him! Crucify Him!"   *Ernaldo Carnutense*

"By carrying in her womb Jesus, the living God, Mary became the Mother of all the living."

                                        St. Irenaeus

Reflection — *"Let us present ourselves to Mary as sinners, for she has pity on those in misery."*

James Alberione

Prayer — "Hail, garden of delights, rich with every flower and all the virtues."   *St. Jerome*

October 31

"Hail, Mary, full of grace, and so replete with grace that you overflow with it for all of us, who are so much in need of grace."   *Bossuet*

"Hail, hidden treasure, fruitful vine, divine spring of purest waters!

"Hail, O silver dove, who bore the long-awaited olive branch of peace to us!

"Hail, fertile mountain, where the Lamb who bore the sins of all the world went to graze.

"Hail, holy mountain, from whom was taken the Stone that destroyed all the statues of idols!"

St. Germanus

Reflection — *"Heaven rejoices, hell trembles, Satan flees every time I say only: 'Hail, Mary!'"*   *St. Bernard*

Prayer — "Hail, ark all of gold, that contained Christ, the Manna of our souls!"

Didimus of Alexandria

NOVEMBER
The Last Things

November 1

All Saints Day—"The fire of purgatory is enkindled by God's love, not by His anger; however, it is still fire." *St. Catherine of Genoa*

"It differs from the fire of hell only in its duration, which is not eternal." *Sts. Thomas and Augustine*

Reflection — *"It is therefore a holy and wholesome thought to pray for the dead (cf. 2 Mc. 12:46). After they have reached heaven, they will become our protectors and save us from perils."*

St. Catherine of Genoa

Prayer — Lord, "make the flames of divine love devour our sins, and thus we will avoid the fires of purgatory." *St. Thérèse of Lisieux*

November 2

All Souls Day—"The most bitter pains of this earth are a gentle breeze in comparison to the pains of purgatory." *St. Catherine of Genoa*

Reflection — *"Tears quickly disappear, and flowers soon wither; only the suffrages we make for the deceased will be of assistance to them."*

St. Augustine

Prayer — O Mary, you are the ark of salvation built by God on the deluge of our faults, so that whoever desires may enter and be saved.

November 3

"Remember your last days, and you will never sin" (Sir. 7:36).*

"Ask yourself often: 'What will this profit me for eternity?' "   *St. Bernard*

Reflection — *We should always increase more and more our devotion to Mary most holy and St. Joseph, the patrons of a good death.*

Prayer — Jesus Master, Way, Truth and Life, have mercy on us!

November 4

"Make certain that if you live a long life, you make amends for your sins and do not increase your faults, instead."   *Imitation of Christ*

Reflection — *"Remember that you are a traveler here on earth. Be on guard as you journey."*

St. Augustine

Prayer — O Mary, who entered the world without sin, from your Son obtain for me the grace to leave this earth free from fault.

November 5

"This slight momentary affliction is preparing for us an eternal weight of glory beyond all comparison" (2 Cor. 4:17).

Reflection — *"If you do not take care of yourself now, who do you want to care for you after your death?"*   *Imitation of Christ*

Prayer — Sacred Heart of Jesus, comforted in Your agony by an angel, comfort me in mine.

November 6

"Who shall dwell on your holy mountain?

He who walks blamelessly...
   who thinks the truth in his heart
   and slanders not with his tongue" (Ps. 15:1-2).*

God said to the souls in purgatory what He said to the unjust servant: "You will never get out till you have paid the last penny" (Mt. 5:26).

Reflection — *"With his angels he can find fault. How much more with those that dwell in houses of clay" (Job 4:18-19).*

Prayer — O Mary, to be devoted to you is a weapon of salvation which God gave to those whom He positively wants to save."

                                   St. John Damascene

November 7

"O terrible moment, on which all eternity depends. All our actions, both good and evil, will scream at us: 'We are your works; we will not abandon you!' " *St. Bernard*

Reflection — *"As long as the day lasts I must carry out the work of the one who sent me; the night will soon be here when no one can work"* (Jn. 9:4).**

Prayer — O Heart of Jesus, convert sinners, save the dying, and free the holy souls from purgatory.

November 8

"God hides from us the knowledge of our last day so that we will live each one of them well.

"Only one thing counts in life: if we obtain it, all is accomplished; if we fail to obtain it, all is lost; it is a good death." *St. Augustine*

Reflection — *"You also must be ready; for the Son of man is coming at an hour you do not expect"* (Mt. 24:44).

Prayer — "O Lord, cut me, burn me now; but do not permit me to be cut off from You and burned in eternity." *St. Augustine*

November 9

"The wages of sin is death. So death spread to all men because all men sinned" (Rom. 6:23, 5:12).

"Of all the holy souls I knew in my lifetime, I saw only three fly directly to heaven immediately after death." *St. Teresa of Avila*

Reflection — *"For those who love God, death is the door to glory; for those who love sin, it is the gateway to ruin."* *St. Augustine*

Prayer — "Jesus Master, Your life is a precept for me—the one safe, true, infallible way. Every other way may be broad and smooth, but it is not Yours.... What You want, I also want. Substitute Your will for mine."
James Alberione

November 10

"You would be glad to be already in the liberty of the glory of the children of God. You would be pleased to be now at your eternal home, and in your heavenly country filled with joy. But that hour is not yet come; for there is yet another time, a time of war, a time of labor and of probation.... Take courage, therefore, and be valiant as well in doing as in suffering things repugnant to your nature."
Imitation of Christ

Reflection — *Let us pray for the dying and ask for ourselves a holy death and the consolation of receiving the last sacraments.*

Prayer — "No one will be saved nor obtain mercy except through you, O heavenly Lady." *St. Germanus*

November 11

Think of the doubts and fears assailing the dying person who must answer to God for his entire life. Reflect upon the confusion in the soul, which is violently attacked by the devil in that decisive hour. Death will separate us from all persons; only one Friend can be near us in that moment: Jesus.

Reflection — '"It is as important to be devoted to Mary as it is to enter heaven, because no one can enter paradise who is not devoted to Mary."

St. Leonard of Port Maurice

Prayer — Mary, Mother of grace and of mercy, defend us from the enemy, and gather us about you at the hour of death!

November 12

"Whoever is enamored of Mary attaches his soul to a steadfast anchor that will draw him to the port of happiness."   *St. John Damascene*

"In reward for her humility, God gave to Mary the power of filling with blessed souls the thrones left empty by the rebellious angels."

St. Louis de Montfort

"Mary is secretary of the King of heaven. It is she who writes in the book of life the names of the predestined and signs them with the emblem of God."   *George de Rhodes*

Reflection — "Whoever loves Mary will always possess a greater abundance of graces.

James Alberione

Prayer — O Mary, our salvation is in your hands. Only watch over us, and we will serve the King. That is, we will serve God!

November 13

"To be greatly devoted to Mary means to possess the keys to God's loveliest treasures."

St. Louis de Montfort

"It is a doctrine preached by all the saints that no grace can come to us from heaven without passing through Mary's hands."

Gerson; St. Alphonsus

"Mary is the fertile valley in which all the beauties of heaven are gathered."   *St. Bernard*

Reflection — *"Remember this well: No one will enter heaven without passing through Mary, as one would pass through a door."*   *St. Bonaventure*

Prayer — O Mary, you read in the mind of God the children whom He calls and for them you have special prayers, light, grace and consolation.

November 14

"Blessed are the dead who die in the Lord... their deeds follow them!" (Rv. 14:13)

The death of the just man is a sweet repose after the struggles of life. "God has put them to the test and proved them worthy to be with him" (Wis. 3:5).**

Reflection — *By leading a holy life, let us make sure that Jesus, the Judge, will receive us kindly, as a father welcomes his son returning from exile.*

Prayer — O Jesus, be not my Judge, but my Savior.

November 15

"So we do not lose heart. Though our outer nature is wasting away, our inner nature is being renewed every day.... We look not to the things that are seen but to the things that are unseen; for the things that are seen are transient, but the things that are unseen are eternal" (2 Cor. 4:16, 18).

Reflection — *The just man, though he dies early, shall be at rest. He has from God the promise to be raised up again (cf. 2 Mc. 7:14).*

Prayer — Free me from eternal death, O Lord, on that terrible day when You will come to judge the world.

November 16

"The Father judges no one, but has given all judgment to the Son" (Jn. 5:22).

"Men's hearts shall tremble with fear as the Judge assembles all to sift for souls who resemble Him."   *Dies Irae*

Reflection — *Let us make a deep examination of conscience: "If we judged ourselves truly, we should not be judged" (1 Cor. 11:31).*

Prayer — "O Jesus, let me serve You in time, so that I may be with You in eternity."

St. Ignatius Loyola

November 17

"The trumpet shall sound loudly, piercing tombs deep in the earth, calling souls to surround His throne."   *Dies Irae*

"For we must all appear before the judgment seat of Christ, so that each one may receive good or evil, according to what he has done in the body" (2 Cor. 5:10).

Reflection — *Life is short; death is certain, but the hour of death is uncertain. I have only one soul; if I lose it, where will I be? If I lose the time I have now, I might not have it at death.*

Prayer — "My God, infinite Purity, I would rather die a thousand deaths than betray You with a single mortal sin."

St. Angela Foligno

November 18

"He [Jesus Christ] will come again with great majesty to judge the living and the dead, and his kingdom will have no end." *Athanasian Creed*

The Lord "will bring to light the things now hidden in darkness, and will disclose the purposes of the heart" (1 Cor. 4:5).

Reflection — *If a virtuous man turns from the path of virtue to do evil, none of his virtuous deeds shall be remembered (cf. Ez. 18:27).*

Prayer — O Lord, "I repeat with the saints: 'Death rather than sin!' 'I prefer to die than stain my soul!' "

St. Stanislaus Kostka

November 19

"He who is not with me is against me, and he who does not gather with me scatters" (Lk. 11:23).

"You who have followed me...will also sit on twelve thrones, judging the twelve tribes of Israel" (Mt. 19:28).

Reflection — *"Flee from sin as from a serpent" (Sir. 21:2).* *

Sin is the enemy who is able to destroy both soul and body in hell.

Prayer — "O God, you are my God whom I seek;
for you my flesh pines and my soul thirsts
like the earth, parched, lifeless and without
water" (Ps. 63:2).*

November 20

"If a man loves me, he will keep my word, and
my Father will love him, and we will come to him
and make our home with him" (Jn. 14:23).

As King, Christ issued laws: "This is my commandment, that you love one another as I have
loved you" (Jn. 15:12).

Reflection — *Consider the wickedness of Herod
who was the first to oppose Jesus, and recall the sorrowful ending he had (cf. Lk. 19:14).*

Prayer — Grant, O Lord, that our death may be
serene, as that of a person faithful to his vocation
in life.

November 21

How loving will God be toward those who have
loved Him with all their heart during life. One
knows that Jesus "will change our lowly body to
be like his glorious body" (Phil. 3:21).

Reflection — *"If the love of God is not enough to
withdraw you from evil, at least the fear of hell
should restrain you."*   *Imitation of Christ*

Prayer — "O Lord, only he who is good, he who
loves You and serves You faithfully and dies in
grace is worthy of heaven."   *Pope St. Pius X*

November 22

As King, Jesus Christ will judge us: "From thence He will come to judge the living and the dead."   *Apostles' Creed*

Reflection — *Jesus is salvation for the good who, by believing in Him, earn paradise; He is damnation to the evil who, by rejecting His doctrine, damn themselves.*

Prayer — Grant our prayer, O Mary, so that all men may accept Jesus Christ, the Divine Master, Way, Truth, and Life, and become docile children of the Catholic Church.

November 23

As King, Jesus Christ will reward the good and punish the wicked: "Come, O blessed of my Father. Depart from me, you cursed" (Mt. 25:34, 41). The sentence will be final and will last for all eternity.

Reflection — *Draw me to Yourself, O Lord. The road is narrow, but it leads to heaven. On the way, I will lean on You, my Guide and my Comfort.*

Prayer — O Lord, grant me a spirit of penance, purity of conscience, hatred for every deliberate venial sin.

November 24

"The death of the just is like the arrival at the house of our dearest Friend or like a leap onto the knees of our Father."   *Elizabeth of Leseur*

Reflection — *"Only he who always seeks to please God in everything is worthy of His peace."*

James Alberione

Prayer — O Mary, gain for yourself the greatest glory: change a great sinner into a great saint.

November 25

No one is as unhappy as the obstinate sinner who heedlessly sleeps in the arms of Satan. Consider the terrible chastisements sent upon Cain, Pharaoh and Saul, because of their obstinacy in their sins.

Reflection — *Obstinacy blinds the mind, hardens the heart, and places the soul in the danger of an impenitent death. Grant me, O Lord, the grace to keep watch on myself, to confess myself often, with the right dispositions.*

Prayer — O Lord, grant me the grace of detaching my heart more and more from all vanity and sinful satisfaction, to seek You only, my supreme and eternal Happiness.

November 26

"I am the way, and the truth, and the life; no one comes to the Father, but by me" (Jn. 14:6).

"He who follows me will not walk in darkness, but will have the light of life" (Jn. 8:12).

Reflection — *"Living in the state of grace means little; it is necessary to live the life of grace by developing it to the fullest blossoming."*   *Pope Pius XI*

Prayer — O Jesus, impress on me, and on every atoning soul, the virtues of Your most holy heart.

November 27

"I am the resurrection and the life;...whoever lives and believes in me shall never die" (Jn. 11:25-26).

"One of the greatest mistakes we can make in our lives is to think so little of heaven."

St. Joseph Cafasso

Reflection — *We live in Christ by remaining in grace, that is, by avoiding mortal sin.*

Prayer — You are with us and from the tabernacle You want to cast light. Grant us true sorrow for sin always.

November 28

How can we prepare for the ineffable bliss of heaven? By keeping close to the Lord: "Our citizenship is in heaven" (Phil. 3:20).

"We show we value God's company when we engage in intimate conversation with Him."

James Alberione

Reflection — *"Let us begin to become more and more attached to prayer. The love of God is shown by desiring and contemplating God, by keeping close to Him."* *James Alberione*

Prayer — "O Jesus, fill me with love for You, contempt for myself, and zeal for others."

Imitation of Christ

November 29

"Heaven! Give me heaven! Such is the yearning of great souls. Who cares about this earth, about pleasures and wealth and honor—give me heaven!"
James Alberione

Reflection — *"Pray to Mary, Queen of Apostles, that she may lift our desires heavenward and with our desires elevate our whole will, too. Pray that she may obtain for all the grace of heavenly wisdom, to be a humble and fervent disciple of Jesus."*

James Alberione

Prayer — O Lord, every day I want to arise to a new life so as to merit to arise in the glory of the last day.

November 30

"Some do desire heaven, but rather half-heartedly, for they never resolve to win it.

"When faced with trying days, remember that what must impart courage is the reward. 'Each will receive his own reward according to his labors' (cf. 1 Cor. 3:8)."
James Alberione

Reflection — *Resolve to choose to die rather than to offend God; even more, resolve to love God above all things until death.*

Prayer — "O Lord, You have created me for Yourself, and for heaven. I know that You will give me all the graces I need to reach heaven.... Lord, I hope in the merits of Your passion and death, and I intend to do good works to earn heaven."

James Alberione

DECEMBER
Humility

December 1

"Take my yoke upon you, and learn from me; for I am gentle and lowly in heart, and you will find rest for your souls. For my yoke is easy, and my burden is light" (Mt. 11:29-30).

"What is humility? Humility is truth. It is thorough self-knowledge, which admits that everything comes to us from God."

James Alberione

Reflection — *"One means of acquiring humility is reading books which treat of it."*　　*James Alberione*

Prayer — Jesus, meek and humble of heart, make my heart like Yours.

December 2

"To him who knocks it will be opened" (Mt. 7:8).

"All the other virtues knock at God's heart, but only humility opens it."　　*St. Augustine*

Reflection — *"God is our Father, and He invites us to pray: 'Ask.' It is up to us to pray and to pray well.*

In the greatness of His heart, our Lord very much desires to grant our requests."   James Alberione

Prayer — "O Jesus Master, You have said: Truly I say to you: whatsoever you shall ask the Father in my name, He will give it to you; so in Your name I ask for victory over my predominant defect. Hear me, O Jesus."   *James Alberione*

December 3

"God opposes the proud, but gives grace to the humble" (Jas. 4:6).

"The Lord can and must listen only to the prayers of the humble. He cannot listen to the prayers of the proud, because all that God does, He does for His glory."   *James Alberione*

Reflection — *"Humility is the secret of receiving graces. God grants many gifts to the humble, while the proud are sent away."*   *James Alberione*

Prayer — O Jesus, may the fire brought by You upon the earth inflame, enlighten, and warm everyone.

December 4

"The humble person, in his conviction that 'we have nothing of our own but lies and sin,' does not hold himself in esteem."   *St. Bernard*

Reflection — *"If you excuse your actions, God will accuse you; but if you accuse yourself, God will excuse you."*   *St. Francis of Assisi*

Prayer — May I know you, O God, to glorify You. And may I know myself to realize my limitations, and to trust in You.

December 5

"My soul proclaims the greatness of the Lord... because he has looked upon his lowly handmaid. Yes, from this day forward all generations will call
me blessed, (Lk. 1:46-48).**

"Mary greatly pleased God because of her virginity; but it was for her humility that she was selected to be His Mother."   *St. Bernard*

Reflection — *"Humility is the root of merit.... One's glory in heaven will be in proportion to one's humility on earth."*   *James Alberione*

Prayer — O Mary, hold me close to you and to your Jesus!

December 6

"Humility is the virtue that captures the heart of God; He remains with the humble like a shadow following a body."   *St. Francis de Sales*

The Lord says:

"This is the one whom I approve:
    the lowly and afflicted man who trembles
        at my word" (Is. 66:2).*

Reflection — *"The prayer to which God listens is the cry of a humble soul, the cry of the needy soul, the expression of one's own inability."* *James Alberione*

Prayer — O Jesus, may I humbly cooperate in Your kingdom.

December 7

"Blessed are the poor in spirit, for theirs is the kingdom of heaven" (Mt. 5:3).

"God chose what is low and despised in the world, even things that are not, so that no human being might boast in the presence of God" (1 Cor. 1:28-29).

Reflection — *"Whoever desires to become great must begin by becoming little."*   St. Augustine

Prayer — O Jesus, pour out an ever greater abundance of grace to sanctify my soul.

December 8

Immaculate Conception—"Mary is called by the angel 'full of grace.' This fullness signifies that she was united to God during her whole life; she was never stained by sin at any time; at the moment in which she left God's creative hands she was already immaculate and holy."   James Alberione

Reflection — *"In order to honor Mary Immaculate, three interior dispositions are necessary: a great horror of sin; great esteem for divine grace; and a deep piety, which reveals itself in the fervent reception of the sacraments of Reconciliation (Penance) and Communion."*   James Alberione

Prayer — Blessed be the holy and Immaculate Conception of the Blessed Virgin Mary, Mother of God.

December 9

"When Jesus had washed their feet, and taken his garments, and resumed his place, he said to them, 'Do you know what I have done to you? You call me Teacher and Lord; and you are right for so I am. If I then, your Lord and Teacher, have washed your feet, you also ought to wash one another's feet. For I have given you an example, that you also should do as I have done to you' " (Jn. 13:12-15).

Reflection — *Jesus continued to teach, "I say to you, a servant is not greater than his master; nor is he who is sent greater than he who sent him. If you know these things, blessed are you if you do them" (Jn. 13:16-17).*

Prayer — Jesus, sole Way of salvation, you invite me: 'Learn from me.' But I resemble you so little!

December 10

"...Christ Jesus, who, though he was in the form of God, did not count equality with God a thing to be grasped, but emptied himself, taking the form of a servant, being born in the likeness of men. And being found in human form he humbled himself and became obedient unto death, even death on a cross" (Phil. 2:5-8).

Reflection — *"Sufferings are the lot we must expect on this earth if we wish to share Jesus Christ's life of poverty, humility, and sacrifice. But then we shall also share in the very merit and glory of our Savior."*   James Alberione

Prayer — Jesus, You pleased the Father; You are my Model.

December 11

"...The disciples came to Jesus, saying, 'Who is the greatest in the kingdom of heaven?' And calling to him a child, he put him in the midst of them, and said, 'Truly, I say to you, unless you turn and become like children, you will never enter the kingdom of heaven. Whoever humbles himself like this child, he is the greatest in the kingdom of heaven' " (Mt. 18:1-4).

Reflection — *"To become as little children means to have a soul as pure as theirs, together with the love and faith that an adult ought to have."*

Cardinal Suhard

Prayer — O Jesus, Divine Master, I thank You for having come down from heaven to free man from so many evils by your teachings, holiness, death and resurrection.

December 12

"A dispute arose among them, which of them was to be regarded as the greatest. And [Jesus] said to them; 'The kings of the Gentiles exercise lordship over them, and those in authority over them are called benefactors. But not so with you; rather let the greatest among you become as the youngest, and the leader as one who serves. I am among you as one who serves" (Lk. 22:24-26, 27).

Reflection — *"Let us often consider our littleness. To be humble we do not need to look for reasons which are more or less true, or which convince us only to some extent. It is enough to think of our last end."*

James Alberione

Prayer — O Divine Master, grant that You may always, everywhere, and in all things dispose of me for Your greater glory.

December 13

"He then spoke this parable addressed to those who believed in their own self-righteousness while holding everyone else in contempt: 'Two men went up into the temple to pray; one was a Pharisee, the other a tax collector. The Pharisee with head unbowed prayed in this fashion: "I give you thanks, O God, that I am not like the rest of men.... I fast twice a week. I pay tithes on all I possess" (Lk. 18:9-11, 12).*

Reflection — *"What a bad habit it is to brag about oneself, repeating over and over to those who want to listen, and to those who do not, the marvels one thinks he has accomplished."*
                                                James Alberione

Prayer – "God, be merciful to me a sinner!" (Lk. 18:13)

December 14

"You are God's chosen race, his saints; he loves you, and you should be clothed in sincere compassion, in kindness and humility, gentleness and patience" (Col. 3:12).**

"Humility is to the other virtues what the links of a chain are to the rosary beads. Without humility other virtues cannot remain together."
                                                St. John Vianney

Reflection — *"There are few humble souls; only those who live in obedience and simplicity are humble."*   James Alberione

Prayer — O Jesus, may I always repeat: "Your will be done."

December 15

"St. Paul wrote: "...A thorn was given me in the flesh, a messenger of Satan to harass me, to keep me from being too elated. Three times I besought the Lord about this, that it should leave me; but he said to me, 'My grace is sufficient for you, for my power is made perfect in weakness.' I will all the more gladly boast of my weaknesses, that the power of Christ may rest upon me" (2 Cor. 12:7-9).

Reflection — *"For the sake of Christ, then, I am content with weaknesses, insults, hardships, persecutions, and calamities; for when I am weak, then I am strong" (2 Cor. 12:10).*

Prayer — O dear Jesus, calm the tempest which reigns in my heart. Grant that I may always take from Your hands all things and thus find perfect peace.

December 16

"I am the vine, you are the branches. He who abides in me, and I in him, he it is that bears much fruit, for apart from me you can do nothing" (Jn. 15:5).

"Humility makes us understand that we are poor sinners and that even after receiving special graces from the Lord we have greatly abused His mercy."   *James Alberione*

Reflection — *"The humble man sees God as the All-Good; in himself he sees the poor sinner. He goes before God as a humble beggar before a rich man, as a child before his good father, as the subject before his king."*   *James Alberione*

Prayer — How good you have been with me, O Lord!

December 17

"The greater you are, the more you should behave humbly, and then you will find favor with the Lord; for great though the power of the Lord is, he accepts the homage of the humble" (Eccl. 3:18-20).**

Reflection — *"God works as He wills. Ask great things, because the humble and greater requests do Him honor."*   *James Alberione*

Prayer — "O God, You are everything. Do not reject me, who am nothing."   *St. Catherine of Siena*

December 18

Jesus, mistreated, insulted and beaten, did not become irritated nor did He rebel.

"He, the meek Lamb, remained silent while His enemies raged at Him."   *St. Augustine*

Reflection — *"Jesus is the Way which we must follow. His life was a series of greater and greater*

*humiliations. O proud soul—we could tell our-
selves—what have you to say, when confronted with
the example of your God?"* James Alberione

Prayer — My crucified Jesus, I hope to obtain pardon through Your most precious blood.

December 19

"As a punishment for the sin of Adam, God
cursed the earth: "Cursed be the ground because
of you!... Thorns and thistles shall it bring forth to
you..." (Gn. 3:17, 18).

"Jesus took upon Himself the thorns, to free us
from the curse." *St. Cyril*

The thorns in Jesus' crown are the sins of pride
and ambition. Jesus, uncreated Wisdom, permitted
Himself to be treated as insane; He, who is all-
powerful pretended to be powerless; He, the most
blessed in heaven, was "...filled with disgrace"
(Lam. 3:30).

Reflection — *"...Clothe yourselves, all of you, with
humility toward one another, for 'God opposes the
proud, but gives grace to the humble.' Humble yourselves therefore under the mighty hand of God, that
in due time he may exalt you" (1 Pt. 5:5-6).*

Prayer — O Jesus, draw me to Yourself, and give
me the grace to imitate You.

December 20

" 'God opposes the proud, but gives grace to
the humble.' Submit yourselves therefore to God.

Resist the devil and he will flee from you.... Humble yourselves before the Lord and he will exalt you" (Jas. 4:6-7, 10).

Reflection — *"There is nothing on earth better than humility. The humble soul is more pleasing, both to God and to men."*   James Alberione

Prayer — Jesus Master, I invoke Your mercy.

December 21

"Do nothing from selfishness or conceit, but in humility count others better than yourselves. Let each of you look not only to his own interests, but also to the interests of others. Have this mind among yourselves which was in Christ Jesus..." (Phil. 2:3-5).

Reflection — *"In His wisdom God gives intelligence to little ones, and how many times we can learn from those who seem to have little talent, but truly possess the spirit of God!"*   James Alberione

Prayer — My God, I make a sacrifice of my whole being to You and join my sacrifice to that of Jesus, my divine Savior.

December 22

"Pride comes first, disgrace comes after;
   with the humble is wisdom found" (Prv. 11:2).**

Reflection — *"If humility is present, even though sins have been committed, the Lord will give the grace to rise again; but if pride is present, even if many years have been spent in the greatest virtue,*

one must always fear. From one moment to another
he could fall into the most humiliating faults."
James Alberione

Prayer — My Jesus, deliver me from the danger
of abusing the gifts You gave me with such
wisdom and love.

December 23

"And the Word became flesh and dwelt among
us, full of grace and truth; we have beheld his
glory, glory as of the only Son from the Father."
(Jn. 1:14).

"Original sin injured the glory of God and
brought sorrow among men. The mystery of Bethlehem restored the glory of God and returned
peace to the world."   *St. Augustine*

Reflection — *"Christ did the will of His Father*
from the beginning of His life to the end. He is our
Model from birth to our last breath—the will of God
always."   *James Alberione*

Prayer — O Jesus, I believe that You are the
Christ, the Son of the living God!

December 24

Caesar Augustus issued an edict, demanding a
census of the entire Empire. Mary and Joseph set
out for Bethlehem, miles and miles away, in obedience to the Emperor's command. After their
tiresome journey, everyone turned them away

from their door because they saw how poor Mary and Joseph were. There was no room for them in the caravan camp.

Reflection — *"Bethlehem's inhabitants rejected Mary and Joseph, and they humbly went away, without a single complaint or one word of bitterness. Let us learn to see the world as it is—full of trickery and malice. Then, we shall not fear the judgments of men nor the world's scorn."*

James Alberione

Prayer — "Do not reject the petitions of us miserable creatures; and deliver us from all dangers, O holy Mother of God."   *James Alberione*

December 25

Christmas—"The Lord himself will give you this sign: the virgin shall be with child, and bear a son, and shall name him Immanuel" (Is. 7:14).*

In the middle of the night, while the world lay in impenetrable silence, the Redeemer was born. Mary wrapped the divine Babe in poor swaddling clothes and adored Him with all her heart, while choirs of angels surrounded Him. The angels sang: "Glory to God in the highest, and on earth peace among men..." (Lk. 2:14).

Reflection — *"Humility is the crib of Jesus; in the humble soul He is born, but He flees from the proud."*   *Timothy Giaccardo*

Prayer — "Only you, O Mary, were found worthy to become the tabernacle of the King of kings."

St. Bernard

December 26

The birth of Christ is the proclamation of God's love for men: "For God so loved the world that he gave his only Son" (Jn. 3:16). Angels brought the glad tidings to the shepherds: "A savior has been born to you" (Lk. 2:11).* The shepherds promptly left their flocks, exclaiming, "Let us go over to Bethlehem!" (Lk. 2:15)*

Reflection — "*After the humble shepherds, there came to the manger the great and the powerful—great men who yet knew how to humble themselves.*"   *James Alberione*

Prayer — "O Christ, You are the King of glory, the eternal Son of the Father, who, in order to save man, did not disdain the womb of a Virgin!"

Te Deum

December 27

"And when the time came for their purification according to the law of Moses, Mary and Joseph brought Jesus up to Jerusalem to present him to the Lord (as it is written in the law of the Lord, 'Every male that opens the womb shall be called holy to the Lord')" (Lk. 2:22-23).

"Mary most holy was not bound by this law because she was always a virgin. Nevertheless, she promptly observed it to practice humility and obedience."   *James Alberione*

Reflection — "*Slaves of our pride, we sometimes sacrifice the most sacred duties and the most noble* *interests, in order to raise ourselves up in public opinion, or out of fear of being derided for doing good works!"*   *James Alberione*

Prayer — "My God, detach my heart from earthly goods, and deeply root it in You, O sole, supreme Good!"   *St. Augustine*

December 28

"But when the time had fully come, God sent forth his Son, born of woman, born under the law, to redeem those who were under the law, so that we might receive adoption as sons.... Through God you are no longer a slave but a son, and if a son then an heir" (Gal. 4:4-6, 7).

Reflection — *"In praying do not heap up empty phrases as the Gentiles do;...your Father knows what you need before you ask him. Pray then like this: Our Father who art in heaven..." (Mt. 6:7, 8-9).*

Prayer — Our Father, who art in heaven, hallowed be Thy name; Thy kingdom come; Thy will be done on earth as it is in heaven. Give us this day our daily bread; and forgive us our trespasses as we forgive those who trespass against us; and lead us not into temptation, but deliver us from evil. Amen.

December 29

Think of the tenderness with which Jesus spoke these words: "Let the children come to me, and do not hinder them; for to such belongs the kingdom of heaven" (Mt. 19:14). Innocent children are a precious treasure for the Church; in fact, "with Baptism, the soul of a child becomes that of an angel."

Lacordaire

Reflection — *"See that you do not despise one of these little ones; for I tell you that in heaven their angels always behold the face of my Father who is in heaven"* (Mt. 18:10).

Prayer — O Jesus, Friend of little ones, bless the children all over the world!

December 30

"Every child is a word of God" and God says nothing but infinitely beautiful things.   *Karl Adam*

How sorrowful is the first sin of an innocent child! It is as if a heavenly spirit had sinned!

Reflection — *"Whoever causes one of these little ones who believe in me to sin, it would be better for him if a great millstone were hung round his neck and he were thrown into the sea"* (Mk. 9:42).

Prayer — O God, to communicate Your love to men, You sent Your only Son, Jesus Christ, into the world. May I learn from Him to love and respect innocence.

December 31

"They came to John, and said to him, 'Rabbi, he who was with you beyond the Jordan, to whom you bore witness, here he is, baptizing, and all are going to him.' John answered..., 'He who has the bride is the bridegroom; the friend of the bridegroom, who stands and hears him, rejoices greatly at the bridegroom's voice; therefore this joy of mine is now full. He must increase, but I must decrease' " (Jn. 3:26-27, 29).

Reflection — *"Continual peace is with the humble; but in the heart of the proud is frequent envy and indignation."*   Imitation of Christ

Prayer — Cleanse me, O Lord, of every sentiment of pride and vanity. Give me humility of heart, so that I may be worthy of Your love.

Daughters of St. Paul

IN MASSACHUSETTS
    50 St. Paul's Ave., Jamaica Plain, Boston, MA 02130;
      617-522-8911; 617-522-0875
    172 Tremont Street, Boston, MA 02111; **617-426-5464;**
      617-426-4230
IN NEW YORK
    78 Fort Place, Staten Island, NY 10301; **212-447-5071**
    59 East 43rd Street, New York, NY 10017; **212-986-7580**
    625 East 187th Street, Bronx, NY 10458; **212-584-0440**
    525 Main Street, Buffalo, NY 14203; **716-847-6044**
IN NEW JERSEY
    Hudson Mall — Route 440 and Communipaw Ave.,
      Jersey City, NJ 07304; **201-433-7740**
IN CONNECTICUT
    202 Fairfield Ave., Bridgeport, CT 06604; **203-335-9913**
IN OHIO
    2105 Ontario St. (at Prospect Ave.), Cleveland, OH 44115; **216-621-9427**
    25 E. Eighth Street, Cincinnati, OH 45202; **513-721-4838**
IN PENNSYLVANIA
    1719 Chestnut Street, Philadelphia, PA 19103; **215-568-2638**
IN VIRGINIA
    1025 King St., Alexandria, VA 22314
IN FLORIDA
    2700 Biscayne Blvd., Miami, FL 33137; **305-573-1618**
IN LOUISIANA
    4403 Veterans Memorial Blvd., Metairie, LA 70002; **504-887-7631;**
      504-887-0113
    1800 South Acadian Thruway, P.O. Box 2028, Baton Rouge, LA 70821
      504-343-4057; 504-343-3814
IN MISSOURI
    1001 Pine Street (at North 10th), St. Louis, MO 63101; **314-621-0346;**
      314-231-1034
IN ILLINOIS
    172 North Michigan Ave., Chicago, IL 60601; **312-346-4228**
      312-346-3240
IN TEXAS
    114 Main Plaza, San Antonio, TX 78205; **512-224-8101**
IN CALIFORNIA
    1570 Fifth Avenue, San Diego, CA 92101; **714-232-1442**
    46 Geary Street, San Francisco, CA 94108; **415-781-5180**
IN HAWAII
    1143 Bishop Street, Honolulu, HI 96813; **808-521-2731**
IN ALASKA
    750 West 5th Avenue, Anchorage AK 99501; **907-272-8183**
IN CANADA
    3022 Dufferin Street, Toronto 395, Ontario, Canada
IN ENGLAND
    128, Notting Hill Gate, London W11 3QG, England
    133 Corporation Street, Birmingham B4 6PH, England
    5A-7 Royal Exchange Square, Glasgow G1 3AH, England
    82 Bold Street, Liverpool L1 4HR, England
IN AUSTRALIA
    58 Abbotsford Rd., Homebush, N.S.W., Sydney 2140, Australia